Introduction to Shipping

Institute of Chartered Shipbrokers

Introduction to Shipping

Published by the

Institute of Chartered Shipbrokers
85 Gracechurch Street, London, EC3V 0AA
United Kingdom

Telephone: +44 20 7623 1111
Email: books@ics.org.uk
www.ics.org.uk

First published 2013
ISBN 978-1-908833-16-7
©Institute of Chartered Shipbrokers 2013

All rights reserved. No part of this publication may be reproduced, stored in a retrieval system or transmitted, in any form or by any means, electronic, mechanical, photocopying, recording or otherwise, without prior permission of the publisher and copyright owner.

Terms of use

While the advice given in this document 'Introduction to Shipping' had been developed using the best information currently available, it is intended purely as guidance to be used at the user's own risk. No responsibility is accepted by the Institute of Chartered Shipbrokers (ICS), the membership of ICS or by any person, firm, corporation or organisation (who or which has been in any way concerned with furnishing of information or data, the compilation or any translation, publishing, supply or sale of the document) for the accuracy of any information or advice given in the document or any omission from the document or for any consequence whatsoever resulting directly or indirectly from compliance with or adoption of guidance contained in the document even if caused by a failure to exercise reasonable care.

Printed and bound in the UK by CPI Group UK, Croydon, CR0 4YY
Artwork Production by Phil McAllister (philmcallisterdesign.com)
Front Cover Image: Portpicturtes.nl
Front cover design by Mark Clubb (www.theclubb.co.uk)

Institute of Chartered Shipbrokers

Acknowledgements

Foreword

Alan Marsh
CEO Braemar Seascope

Shipping is the biggest industry in the world. This is a bold statement, but one that I will attempt to justify.

Before a ship is built, the naval architects and the classification societies discuss the design with the ship owner. That's three sectors.

Shipping markets are studied which will involve shipbrokers. These may also be involved in negotiations with a shipyard. Early in the peace, banks will be involved; many having large ship finance departments. A new-building order is placed with a shipyard. We are now up to six.

The shipyard will buy steel from steelmakers, engines from engine makers, wiring, navigation and radar equipment, winches, ropes, paint and varnish, windows, portholes, hydraulics, furnishings, cooking equipment and all the other thousands of suppliers who are involved in the building and the fitting out of a ship. We must be up to 50 industry sectors by now, employing hundreds of thousands of staff.

The vessel must be manned by officers and crew. There are about 100,000 sea-going ships trading, probably with an average of 20 personnel on board plus half as many again who may be on leave or undergoing training ashore. That is three million people. Then there are the training colleges and the recruitment companies.

When the ship is ready to be delivered, there is a ship's agent, ship's pilot, bunker suppliers and tugs to tow the ship out to the sea. There are the navigation marks which someone has to manufacture and put in place. There are the chart-makers who put on paper where these marks are and the channels they guard. The underwriters and other insurance employees are also closely involved. PandI Clubs also put in their share of hard work.

Our new ship goes to load a cargo at a port. There are the port authorities, pilots, tugs, linemen, berthing masters, ship's agents, customs and immigration officials, port state inspectors and coastguards. There are 835 active seaports in the world plus several thousand smaller ports which have differing amounts of activity. We are entering the realms of the uncountable in terms of emplpyed persons.

And we have not counted the canal workers, the dredgers and the maintenance personnel as well as the crane builders and other cargo handling equipment. We have also omitted the people who bring cargoes to the ports such as barge crews plus people who manage the infrastructure around the port.

Of cargoes carried around the world, in excess of 95pct of manufactured goods as well as raw materials such as oil, ore, grain and gas are transported by sea. This went largely unrecognised until pictures in the media showed baby's nappies, powdered milk and high-powered motor bikes spilling out of broached containers onto a beach following the beaching of a container ship a few years ago.

We also have to consider those who manage the ships from on shore: Ship managers and cargo suppliers and all those back room support staff. And last but not least, those who train them. We are now discussing those highly proficient personnel such as those who work directly or indirectly for the Institute of Chartered Shipbrokers. And we are not finished there. Disputes may arise which may be settled by arbitrators, by admiralty lawyers or by the courts of law. There are also the law-makers such as those at the IMO.

So when I say shipping is the biggest industry in the world, who can point out a bigger one? Oh and then there are the dockyards – enough said, I think. Apart from one or two highly-publicised incidents, the fact that this is mainly an invisible industry which does not register on most people's radar, is a tribute to its success.

Foreword

Acknowledgements

First and foremost we would like to thank Alan Marsh of Braemar Seascope for his support and encouragement in the revision of this book. We must also acknowledge the contribution of several industry professionals, but special thanks are due to Bridget Hogan.

Also special thanks to Simon Sharp for his efforts to update the contents of the book.

The illustrations have been sourced from across the industry but with particular thanks to Danny Cornelissen of Port Pictures NL and Alexander Kopylov of Indeheit Ltd. The artistry of their images raises the stakes in the appearance and presentation of maritime text books.

Contents

Chapter 1: Basic geography, the oceans and the seas

1.1	The oceans	2
1.2	The seas	2
1.3	Shallows and deeps	2
1.4	Currents	3
1.5	Storms	5
1.6	Ports	7
1.7	Tidal influences	8
1.8	Flattening the world	8

Chapter 2: The ship

2.1	Introduction	12
2.2	Crossing water dry-shod	12
2.3	Sail to steam	13
2.4	Early cargoes	14
2.5	Expansion of trade	14
2.6	Specialised vessels	15
2.7	Tanker trades	17
2.8	Gas carriers	17
2.9	Introduction of containers	18
2.10	Sub-sea oil developments	19
2.11	Fleet expansion	21
2.12	Tonnage and loadlines	21

Chapter 3: Modern shipping and trade

3.1	Why trade grew	26
3.2	Bulk shipping growth	27
3.3	Crude oil and products	28
3.4	Gas carriers	29
3.5	Development of containers	30
3.6	Offshore	32
3.7	Big is better!	34

Chapter 4: The port

4.1	Introduction	38
4.2	Getting cargoes afloat	38
4.3	Gateway	38
4.4	Infrastructure	39
4.5	Special ports	40
4.6	Multi cargo ports	45

Contents

Chapter 5: Essential ingredients for the shipping cake

5.1	Traditional ship-owner	50
5.2	Modern ship-owner	50
5.3	Get a ship	50
5.4	Classification Societies	51
5.5	Naval Architect	53
5.6	Shipbuilders	53
5.7	Ship equipment manufacturers	53
5.8	Port workers	54
5.9	Ships Agents	56
5.10	Cargo handling	56
5.11	Insurers	57
5.12	Protection and Indemnity Club (P&I Club)	57
5.13	Marine Surveyors	59

Chapter 6: Ship Management

6.1	Ship management	62
6.2	Third-party management	62
6.3	Crew management	62
6.5	Commercial management	63

Chapter 7: Back office support

7.1	Shipbrokers	66
7.2	Bunker suppliers	67
7.3	Admiralty law	68
7.4	Arbitrators	69
7.5	Chart developers	70

Chapter 8: Law makers, regulators and enforcers

8.1	The International Maritime Organization (IMO)	74
8.2	US Congress	76
8.3	Flag State	77
8.5	Port State Officials	78
8.6	Port state inspectors	78

Contents

Chapter 9: Law of carriage

9.1	Introduction	82
9.2	Fundamentals of english law	82
9.3	Arbitration	83
9.4	The contract	83
9.5	Remedies for breach of contract	84
9.6	Tort	84
9.7	Contracts relating to the carriage of goods by sea	85
9.8	Liner bills of lading	86
9.9	The hague/visby rules	87
9.10	Himalaya clause	88
9.11	The hamburg rules	89
9.12	The rotterdam rules	89
9.13	Agency	90
9.14	Breach of warranty of authority	90
9.15	Protection and indemnity associations	91

Chapter 10: Where the money comes from

10.1	Introduction	94
10.2	Types of employment	100

Chapter 11: Accounts

11.1	Introduction	104
11.2	Accounting	104
11.3	Capital	104
11.4	Credit	105
11.5	Management accounting	106
11.6	Cash flow	106
11.7	Costs	107
11.8	Types of companies	108
11.9	Exchange rates	109
11.10	Company accounts	110

Chapter 12: On board ship

12.1	Ship's officers	112
12.2	Deck officers	112
12.3	Manning	113
12.4	International crews	114
12.5	Application of regulations	114
12.6	A day in the life of a mariner	115

Chapter 13: Maintenance and demolition

13.1	Dry docks	120
13.2	Why a ship comes to the end of its working life	120
13.3	Breaker's yards	121

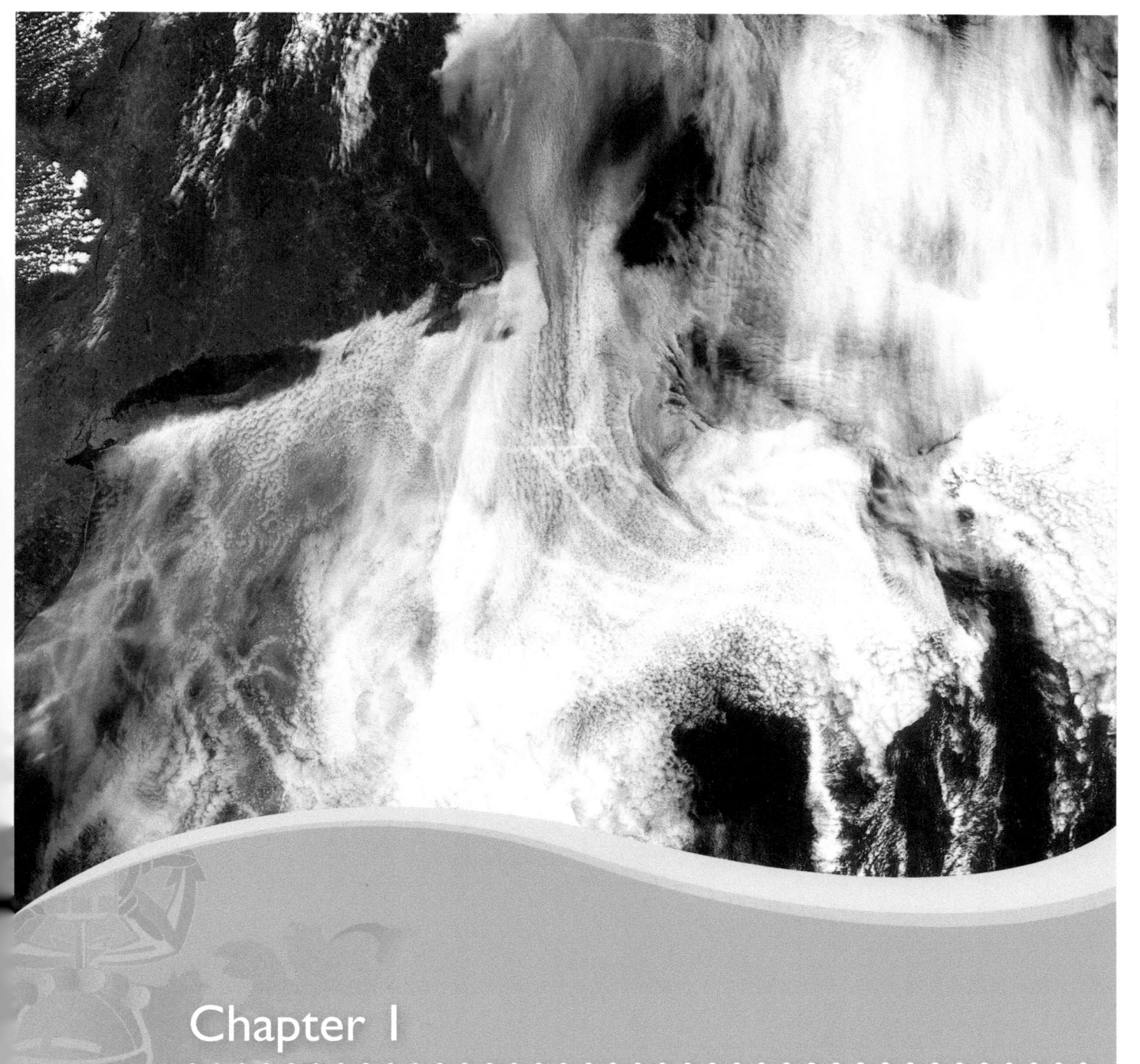

Chapter 1
Basic geography, the oceans and the seas

Florida coast from space

Chapter 1

1.1　THE OCEANS

There is only one global ocean. But the seas are geographically divided into what may be described as sub-oceans. These are the Atlantic Ocean, the Pacific Ocean, the Indian Ocean, the Arctic Ocean and the Southern or Antarctic Ocean.

These five oceans are not separate bodies of water. Each is part of one continuous oceanic mass. Boundaries between the oceans were gradually decided upon internationally for a variety of reasons. Some were geographical, some historical and some were agreed for scientific purposes.

The major ones are the Indian Ocean, the Atlantic and the Pacific. Because of their size, the Pacific and Atlantic were divided into North and South. The Southern Ocean is the most-recently agreed ocean. Its boundaries were set in 2000 by the International Hydrographic Organization.

From a shipping viewpoint, the North Atlantic and the North Pacific are the busiest stretches with the East-West trade routes running across them. The Indian Ocean comes a close third.

The world's oceans

The lesser-used oceans are the South Pacific, the South Atlantic, the Southern and the Arctic.

1.2　THE SEAS

For geographic ease, the oceans have areas of them designated as seas. For example the South China Sea is part of the Pacific; the Red Sea and the Arabian Sea are included in the Indian Ocean area. The Caribbean Sea lies within the boundaries of the Atlantic.

The Mediterranean is a special case. Before the Suez Canal was built, the only major entrance and exit for both the Mediterranean and the Black Seas was the Strait of Gibraltar. They can therefore be viewed as semi-landlocked although they form major maritime highways.

1.3　SHALLOWS AND DEEPS

The oceans comprise large areas of extremely deep saline water. They cover close to 71% of the world's surface area. The average water depth is about 3,750 metres or 12,500 feet. The total volume is approximately 310m cubic miles. The deepest part is the Marianas Trench in the Western Pacific to the East of the Mariana Islands of which the island of Guam forms a part. The trench is about 1,500 nautical miles long and about 40 wide. At the southern end is the Challenger Deep where the maximum known depth is 10,910 metres. Unconfirmed soundings have been measured at more than 11,000 metres or 36,000 feet.

For comparison purposes, the Himalayan range of mountains stretch about the same distance. It has nine of the highest mountains in the world. Mount Everest is 8,848 metres above sea level or about 29,000 feet. It would be possible to fit the whole mountain range into the Marianas Trench.

1.4 CURRENTS

Oceans experience large movements of water. The main ones are the ocean currents. The ones that move away from the equator towards the poles are warm currents. Those that move towards the equator from the north or the south are cold currents. They move around the land masses which are called continents.

Ocean currents – a vertical view.

It can be seen that in the Atlantic the swirling current moving North-east represents the Gulf Stream. It travels along the surface down to about 400m water depth. When it arrives off the coast of Norway, it cools, becomes denser and sinks towards the ocean floor. It then moves in a South-easterly direction down the coast of North America. It affects the climate to such an extent that Europe's West coast is considerably warmer than the equivalent latitude on the Canadian and American East coasts.

In the South Pacific there is an anti-clockwise ocean current. It travels from the Antarctic, up the West coast of South America. This cold current is called the Humboldt. It keeps sea temperatures low, but it gradually warms as it moves towards the tropics. Here it travels West towards Australia and bends down back towards the Antarctic.

Currents affect passage planning even in these days of powerful ocean-going ships. The Southerly Agulhas current flows from the Mozambique Channel, down the East coast of South Africa. It has a powerful flow of up to five knots in some cases.

It has the effect of forcing ship's Masters to pursue a Northerly course up the South African coast and to hug the shore. Many a ship has run aground trying to maintain a good speed against the current.

Chapter 1

General-purpose cargo ship BBC China aground off the coast of South Africa after trying to avoid the Agulhas current.

Because of the turbulent nature of weather conditions off South Africa, early navigators named it the Cape of Storms. Portuguese officials ordered the named changed to Cape of Good Hope, to encourage navigators to find a sea route to India despite its strong currents.

Another threat posed to vessels close to the Agulhas current is that of rogue waves which grow and are drawn towards areas where warm ocean currents flow.

The tanker Wilstar lost its bow off the South African coast.

The rogue wave phenomena is little understood. Seasoned American sailor Joshua Slocum discussed his encounter when sailing in the warm southbound Brazil current and its rogue waves in his book, *Sailing Alone Around the World*, published in 1889:

Basic geography, the oceans and the seas

My ship passed in safety Bahia Blanca, also the Gulf of St. Matias and the mighty Gulf of St. George. Hoping that she might go clear of the destructive tide-races, the dread of big craft or little along this coast, I gave all the capes a berth of about fifty miles, for these dangers extend many miles from the land. But where the sloop avoided one danger she encountered another. For, one day, well off the Patagonian coast, while the sloop was reaching under short sail, a tremendous wave, the culmination, it seemed, of many waves, rolled down upon her in a storm, roaring as it came. I had only a moment to get all sail down and myself up on the peak halyards, out of danger, when I saw the mighty crest towering masthead-high above me. The mountain of water submerged my vessel. She shook in every timber and reeled under the weight of the sea, but rose quickly out of it, and rode grandly over the rollers that followed. It may have been a minute that from my hold in the rigging I could see no part of the Spray's hull. Perhaps it was even less time than that, but it seemed a long while, for under great excitement one lives fast, and in a few seconds one may think a great deal of one's past life. Not only did the past, with electric speed, flash before me, but I had time while in my hazardous position for resolutions for the future that would take a long time to fulfill.

1.5 STORMS

Winds also affect commercial shipping, but these are almost exclusively those of a severe nature. Tropical revolving storms (TRS) occur during defined periods of the year. The hurricane season on the US East coast occurs between June and September, although some rogue storms are spawned earlier and some later.

Similarly in Southeast Asia, typhoons occur from May to November but are especially prevalent in September. These storms develop in tropical areas and head West and North. In the case of the USA and the Caribbeans, storms are conceived when sea temperatures near the Cape Verde Islands rise above 82°F. Winds start to revolve anti-clockwise around a low pressure area and head for land in the West growing in size and height, developing severe winds and gathering up moisture. Wind speeds well in excess of 64 knots develop.

In Asia, storms are spawned to the East of the Marianas Islands. The Philippine Islands are usually the first to be hit. The storm then moves Northwest. Early in the typhoon season storms tend to head in the direction of Singapore and Vietnam. Later they head towards Hong Kong and the Chinese mainland. In the autumn they target Taiwan and Japan.

Elsewhere in the world, Indian Ocean storms hit the Bay of Bengal where they are called cyclones or cyclonic storms. In reality severe storms occur worldwide where local conditions conspire in a typical way to produce deep low pressure areas which need to be filled from high pressure areas. This pressure imbalance causes the typically powerful winds and heavy rainfall.

Chapter 1

Hurricane Andrew hit the Bahamas and Florida in 1997.

The record amount of rainfall in a storm was experienced on the island of Réunion on the 15th and 16th March 1952. 1,870mm of rain fell in 24 hours. The island also holds the record for the most rainfall in 72 hours. In March 2007, the tropical storm Gamede dropped 3,929mm in three days. For those more conversant with imperial measurements, this is 12 feet 9 inches of rain.

There are well-proven ways for shipping to avoid the damaging high winds towards the centre of a TRS. In the northern hemisphere, stand facing the wind. The eye of the storm will lie 90° to ones right. The navigator keeps the wind on the ship's starboard bow and the vessel will steer away from the dangerous storm centre. In the southern hemisphere, the opposite applies.

Some harbours in storm-prone areas have typhoon anchorages or specially designed buoys capable of withstanding the enormous pull of a ship under the pressure of storm force winds, where humans cannot stand upright.

In the absence of such facilities, Masters are usually advised to head out to sea, to gain plenty of sea room and ride out the crisis. It is uncomfortable but modern ships are designed to survive such extremes of weather.

Basic geography, the oceans and the seas

Vessel navigating in smooth seas

1.6 PORTS

Ships trade between places where they are protected from extremes of weather. These are called ports. In size they vary from cities such as Singapore and Shanghai in the East and London and New York in the West at the top of the size range to small ports or rivers which are only accessible to small craft. It is a good exercise to study maritime atlases and learn where the major and some of the less major ports are located.

In the maritime press, shipping contracts, called fixtures are recorded and if ports or regions are mentioned, a quick glance at the map will quickly fix the position of these in the student's memory. It is also useful to study where various shipping canals are situated and calculate what difference in mileage using them makes to a ship's trade.

1.7 TIDAL INFLUENCES

Another influence on ships at sea and in port is that of tides. Tidal flow is a complicated subject, but is simply explained. Tides are the rise and fall in sea levels caused by the gravitational pull of the moon and to a lesser extent, the sun. When these two influences are acting together the rises and falls are extreme and are called spring tides. When they are acting against each other, the tidal range is less and are called neap tides

1.8 FLATTENING THE WORLD

From space, planet Earth is shown in its true round shape. But in the maritime field it is represented by different projections which distort the sphere to make it appear flat. The most common projection is the Mercator Projection.

To understand its design, it is important to study the artificial grid lines marked on a map or chart. The vertical lines which run from the North Pole to the South are called Meridians of Longitude. The lines which are drawn from East to West are called Parallels of Latitude. The former are marked out in degrees of Longitude from nought to 180 degrees. They are measured both East and West from the Greenwich Meridian which is the internationally-accepted Primary Meridian, close to London.

As an example, New York is close to the 74° West Meridian; Hong Kong is close to 114° East. In terms of Latitude, New York lies close to the 41st parallel of Latitude or 40° 45' North (of the equator). Montevideo is close to the 35th parallel South. As a result of these arbitrary lines, a position can be marked on a chart.

In a Mercator Projection, the earth is stretched cylindrically. It is then opened up and stretched out to represent a flat surface. There is little distortion at the equator but further north and south comparative sizes are anomalous. For instance Greenland looks the same size as South America, whereas in reality South America is far larger.

The importance of this projection is that lines drawn on such a map always meet the meridians at the same angle. Thus ship's courses can be drawn with the angle being recorded in degrees.

Mercator projection.

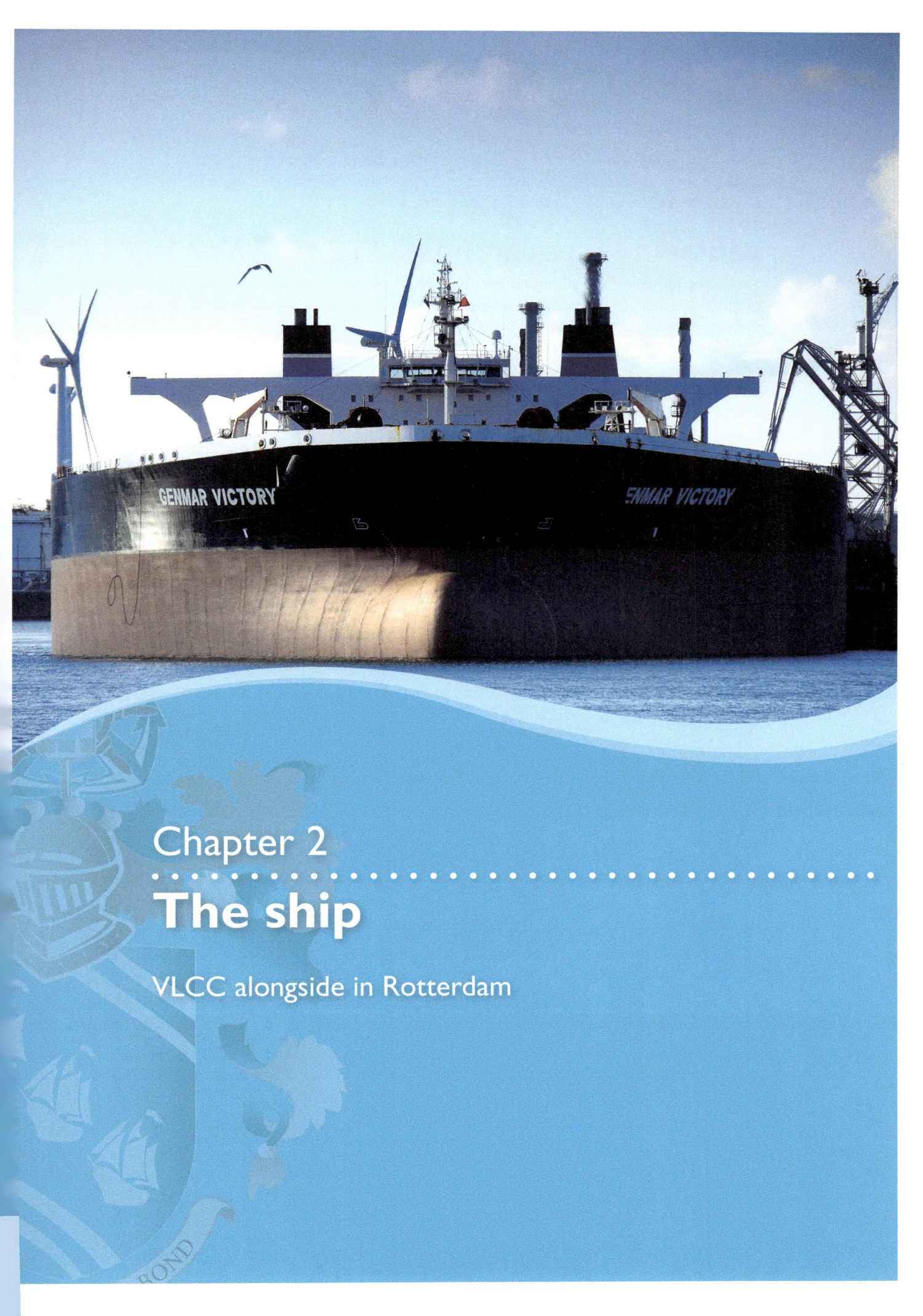

Chapter 2
The ship

VLCC alongside in Rotterdam

Chapter 2

2.1 INTRODUCTION

A ship is a man-made object designed with sufficient buoyancy to enable it to float upon water. By tinkering with the length, the breadth and depth of the object and the materials with which it is made, it can be altered to take a load on board and still remain afloat.

2.2 CROSSING WATER DRY-SHOD

The human animal has refused to be hemmed in by barriers. They have always torn down, climbed over or crossed them. When confronted with a stream they have waded across. When it was too deep they swam across. When they wanted to remain dry they crossed on a buoyant log using poles for propulsion. They dug the centre out of the logs to make them lighter and easier to manoeuvre. In a new direction they made frameworks of sticks covered with animal hides. This led to birch-bark canoes and rafts. There was no end to human ingenuity. Each challenge threw up a new solution.

Coracle

Imagine the Turkish Strait, which divides present day Istanbul, without bridge or boat. To travel from the southern suburbs of the city to the northern suburbs would take a journey around the perimeter of the Black Sea taking many weeks or even months.

Imagine citizens in Roman times having to walk upstream from the city of Rome to the nearest ford on the River Tiber to cross over to the other bank.

And in what is present-day Philippines, without boats, the population of Mindoro would have subsisted on locally-grown produce and locally-hunted animals without being able to travel to Mindanao or Panay; and taking fish from the sea could only be accomplished from the beach.

The Chinese would have been hemmed in by their great rivers such as the Yangtze and the Hanjiang. To reach the lowest crossing point would have required a march of many days.

Ancient scripts have described 'those that go down to the sea in ships and exercise their business in great waters.' Thus the evolution of ships has followed the evolution of humankind. Travel and

The ship

transport by boat and ship grew from stream to river, to estuary and to short sea. Eventually humans braved the elements to make their journeys even longer and further from shore.

Ships evolved from galleasses powered by oars to longboats and galleons powered by sail.

2.3 SAIL TO STEAM

For many centuries mariners were forced to ply their profession at the beck and call of wind and tide. Ship's rigs were tweaked and hulls redesigned to gain more control over the course and speed of their ships, but little headway was made.

When the industrial revolution was well underway and the use of steam power became more widespread, the possibility of greater flexibility in the shipping industry was opened up. Coal-fired steam vessels increased the geographical scope of trade. The shipping family tree grew a second branch.

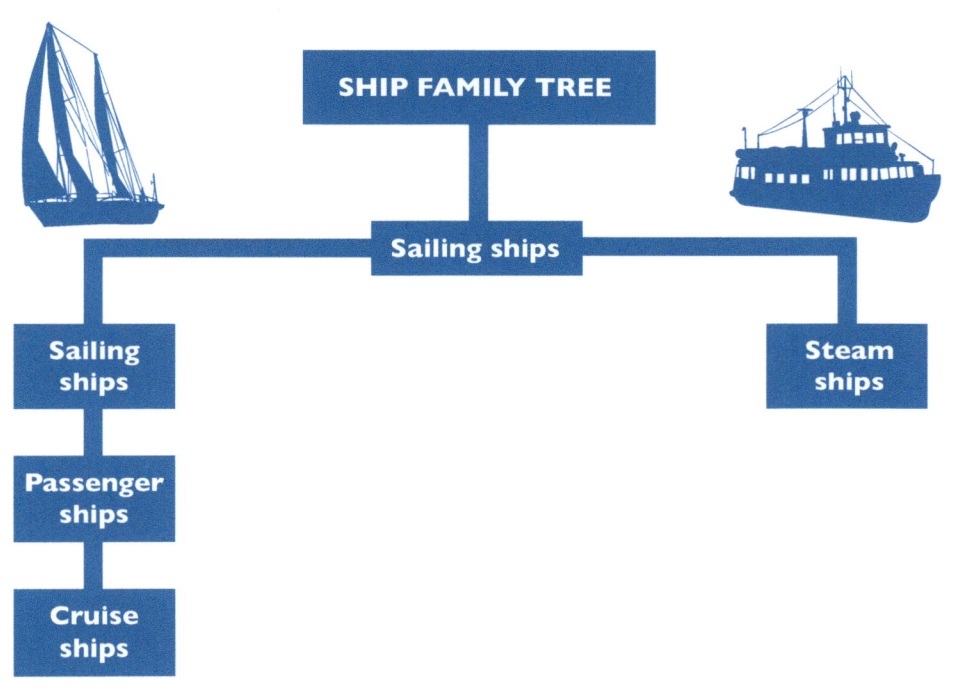

Whereas in the past, sailing ships were of a similar universal layout, the introduction of steam-powered ships allowed for more specialised designs to cater for specific cargoes. Coal started to be carried in bulk and the bulk grain trade started.

2.4 EARLY CARGOES

These pioneers did meet with various setbacks. Shippers found out by bitter experience that coal needed special stowage and ventilation if it was not to explode. It was discovered that bulk grain flowed like water and seriously affected a ship's stability.

These and other mishaps laid the foundations for international directives such as the loadline, the coal and the grain regulations.

Chapter 2

The world as seen by sixteenth century geographers

Increased international demand for oil sent naval architects in a different direction as specialised oil tankers were developed. And so the shipping family tree grew a third limb.

2.5 EXPANSION OF TRADE

Great Britain's industrial revolution created a demand for its products overseas, into Europe and into the British Empire which by then covered half the globe. High grade iron ore and coking coal was shipped into the country's industrial heartland.

Cotton mills were fed by raw cotton from the USA and Egypt and thermal coal was imported to fire up their boilers. There was a move from agriculture to industry and imports of food grew. Trade volumes soared.

The ship

Early oil tanker 'Donax'.

The commercial tonnage supply fell into three distinct groups: Dry cargo ships, tankers and miscellaneous types such as passenger ships, ferries, fishing boats, tugs and dredgers.

BP Tanker British Sovereign

2.6 SPECIALISED VESSELS

As markets developed and the scope and variety of dry cargoes grew, so ships became more specialised; different types and classes were built. Small bulk carriers rubbed shoulders with tweendeckers and insulated ships carrying chilled and frozen foods such as meat, fruit and vegetables.

Chapter 2

'Devonia' changed from troop ship to school cruise vessel.

Fast mail ships hosting hundreds of passengers and parcels of freight plied the oceans sharing them with liners on dedicated trade routes which carried just a few passengers. By the 1960s aeroplanes encroached on merchant ship territory for passengers and mail, but cargo was little affected

Panama Canal from space

2.7 TANKER TRADES

Tanker demand also grew as ships burned oil instead of coal and the use of road vehicles spread worldwide.

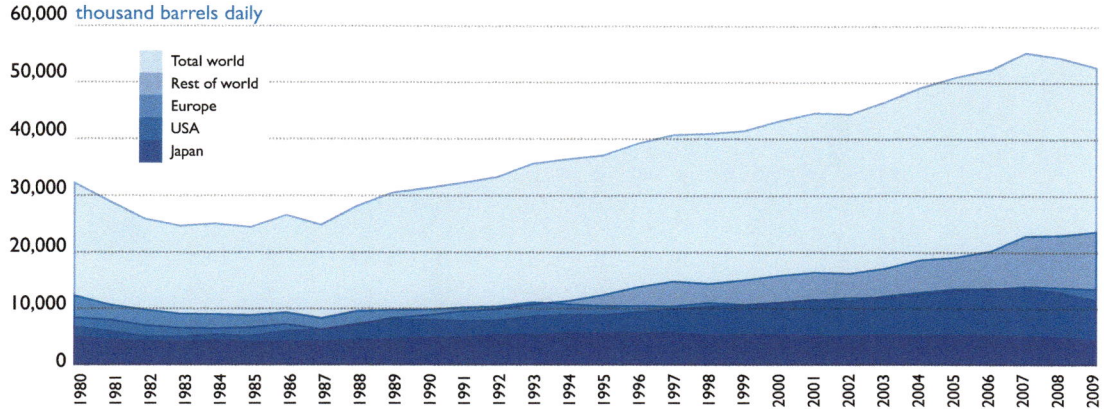

Fig 1. World tanker trade growth – From BP Statistical review of World Energy

But right up to the 1960s tanker designs were very similar. On the whole, crude oil tankers grew slightly larger but fuel oils and clean refined products were carried in smaller ships of 16-20,000-dwt. This state of affairs continued until the development of cargo tank coatings allowed the sub-division of the smaller segments of the tanker market into dirty and clean sectors.

In the dirty sector over the next couple of decades, recognisable tanker sizes emerged; VLCCs, Suezmax, Aframax, Panamax and MRs.

During the same period, the clean branch sub-divided into clean petroleum products and petrochemicals as well as vegetable oils and suchlike with usual ship sizes settling in at around the 30-45,000-dwt size.

And so the die was cast for the establishment of tanker market segments and the shipping tree spread its branches further.

2.8 GAS CARRIERS

An offshoot of the mainstream tanker sector was the gas carrier trade. The oil refining process produced liquid petroleum gases (LPG), such as butane and propane. These were used in the production of industrial chemicals and fertilisers. They were also used for cooking and heating in remote areas and tankers were designed to transport them. They were to all intents and purposes large floating camping gas cylinders.

Chapter 2

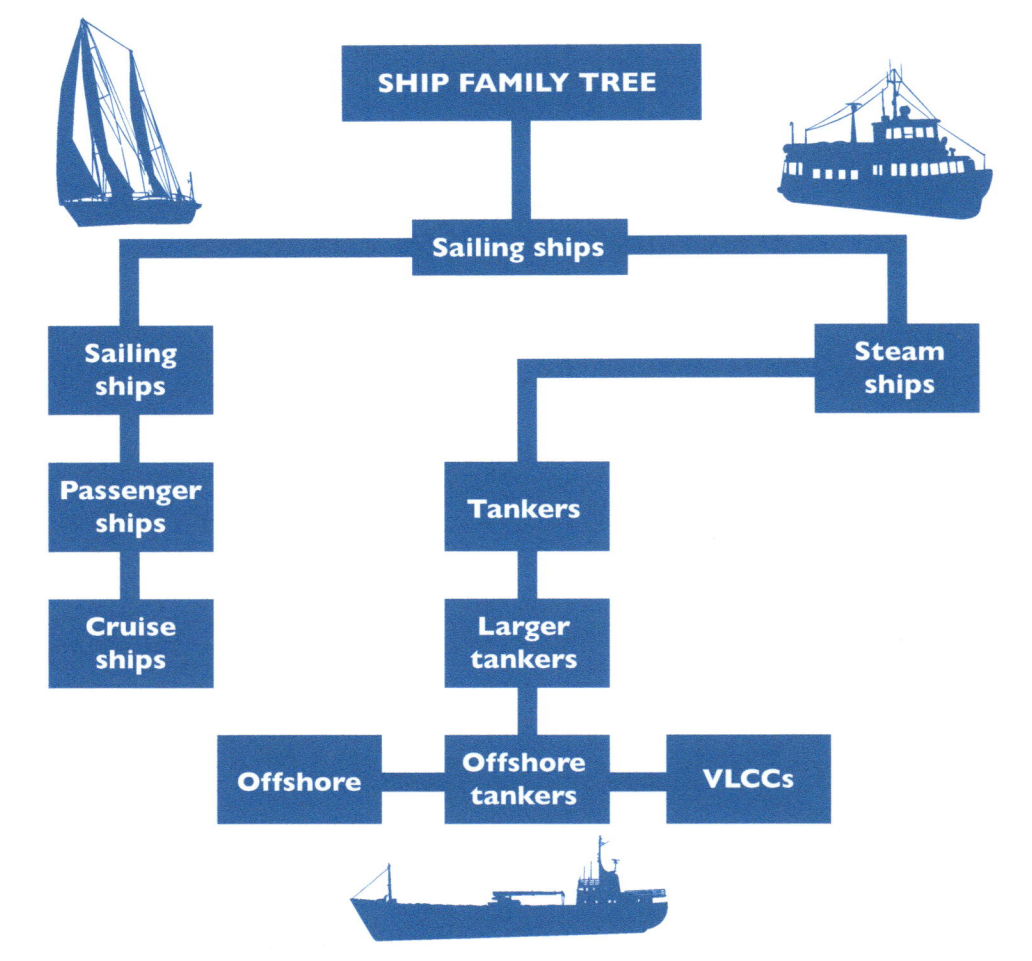

Natural gas was also used for similar purposes and it was found that by cooling the gas to -160deg C, it shrunk in volume by 500-fold. If maintained at this temperature it could be transported in heavily insulated tankers to its markets. The sizes of gas carriers have also increased enormously over the years.

2.9 INTRODUCTION OF CONTAINERS

On the dry side, the size of cargo liners remained largely unchanged at around the 12,000-dwt mark. Until that is, Malcolm McLean introduced the cargo container into the mix on the North American coast in the 1960s. Containerisation had the advantage of reducing ship's port time by obviating the need for traditional stevedoring work of loading and unloading at the docks.

Dedicated container ships quickly took over from traditional cargo liners and they grew in size from 1,000-teu or about 14,000-dwt, to their current maximum size of 15,000-teu or 157,000-dwt. They also increased in speed from about 15-knots to more than 25.

The ship

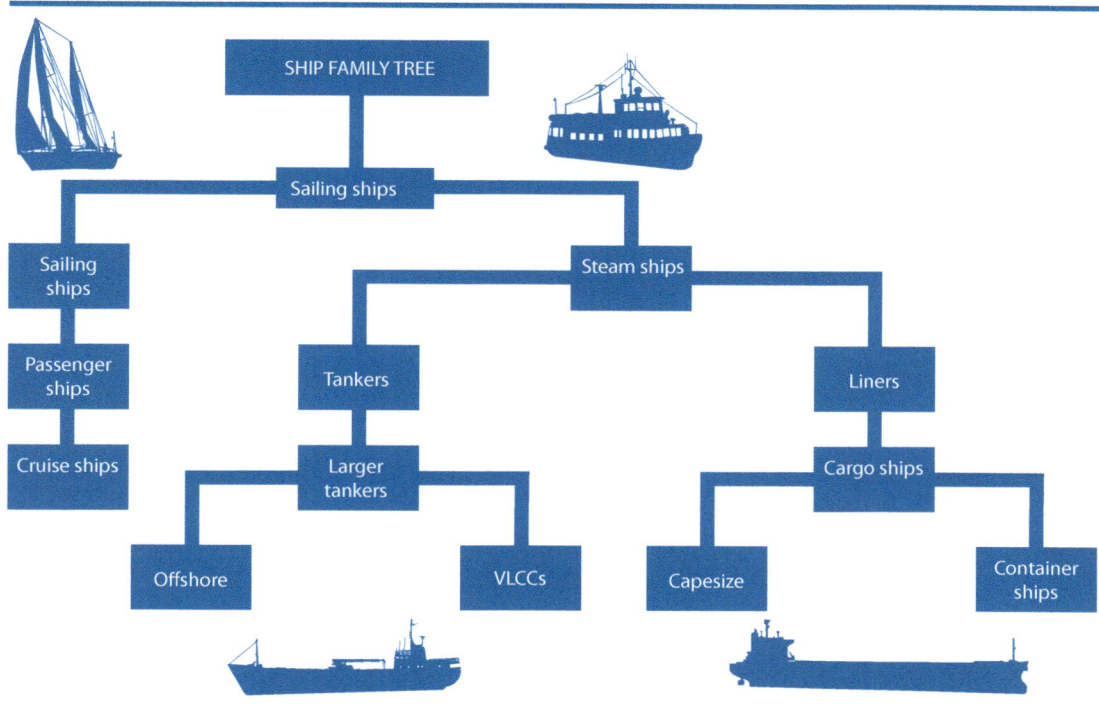

This transformation of the liner trade allowed more size-specific trades within the dry-bulk sector. The largest volumes of cargoes such as coal and iron ore were carried in the largest of bulk carriers. Smaller volumes such as grain and other mineral ores and iron ores carried to draught-restricted ports were lifted in Panamax bulkers. Smaller volume cargoes such as wood-chips, timber and steels were traded in Supramaxes, Handymaxes and Handysizes.

2.10 SUB-SEA OIL DEVELOPMENTS

Booming trade and rising world GDP put pressure on existing land-based oil reserves. The rise of OPEC persuaded the larger consumers to seek out and develop new oilfields in less politically-volatile areas. Large reservoirs were discovered in Alaska and in the North Sea and West Africa also benefited from this push for energy sources far removed from the Middle East.

Many of these new discoveries were on land, but exploration in the North Sea opened up a new type of business venture, the offshore oil industry. Exploration platforms were towed into place and anchored to the seabed. Production platforms were placed over oil finds while pipelines joined oil fields together to get the oil ashore.

Chapter 2

'Far Scorpion' offshore anchor-handling tug.

Some discoveries such as the Forties field took oil to the surface and with the aid of specially-designed tankers ran a shuttle service to shore tanks in the Shetland Islands.

But all these hundreds of installations and thousands of oil workers required support. And this came in the form a large fleet of offshore support vessels. The inhospitable weather conditions sharpened the maritime industry's knowledge and understanding of the design requirements for such vessels. And it has spawned a huge fleet of supply boats, tug boats, anchor-handling tugs, pipelaying barges and many more designs.

The industry has spread globally with offshore exploration taking place off every continent except the Antarctic. And no longer was the oil industry restricted to continental shelves. Deepwater drilling in places such as the Gulf of Mexico in water depths of nearly 10,000 feet are becoming commonplace.

The ability to drill in such water depths has led to the detection of huge oil fields such as those in the Compos and Santos basins in the South Atlantic off Brazil which in size are thought to match the giant discoveries made in Saudi Arabia.

2.11 FLEET EXPANSION

And so the shipping industry has risen from humble beginnings to a huge industry. It is difficult to identify the numbers of ships sailing our seas and rivers. It depends on how one defines a ship. But according to London shipbroker Clarksons, the 2012 worldwide fleet comprised 58,040 vessels. It also recorded that a further 5,409 were being built or had been ordered. So the huge worldwide fleet is set to grow even bigger.

Ship Type	Numbers in Fleet	Numbers on Order
Oil tankers under 10,000-dwt	3,967	559
Oil tankers over 10,000-dwt	5,049	116
Chemical tankers	3,680	258
Other tankers	646	35
Bulkers	8,890	2,387
LPG	1,217	78
LNG	373	58
Container ships	5,093	623
Multi-purpose ships	3,053	352
General cargo ships	15,329	117
RoRo	2,263	55
Car carriers	714	49
Refrigerated vessels	1,744	1
Offshore support vessels	5,207	692
Others	815	19
Total Fleet	**58,040**	**5,409**

Fig 2. Numbers of ships above 1,000dwt as at 1st January 2012. Data from Clarksons Research, London. 2012.

2.12 TONNAGE AND LOADLINES

When describing a ship it is quite common to hear people state that it is "so many tons" and leave it at that. In fact in shipping the word ton, or the metric equivalent tonne has many different meanings and ways of being calculated.

There are two distinct areas where the word ton is used. One is a measurement of volume or space ton. These are used to measure the carrying capacity of a ship and usually translate into nett tonnage and gross tonnage. They are used to levy port dues on a ship.

Despite world-wide discussion and agreement on NT and GT, the Suez Canal and the Panama Canal authorities decided to retain their respective unique methods of measuring ships for the purpose of calculating canal charges.

Chapter 2

2.12.1 Displacement Tonnage

This is the actual weight of the ship and the word displacement is used in reference to Archimedes Law, which states that the weight of a body is equal to the weight of water it displaces

Light Displacement

Is the actual weight of the empty ship, which is of interest to technical people and also to ship sale and purchase brokers when negotiating the sale of a ship to the scrap trade since it is a measure of the quantity of steel and a few other metals that are being sold.

Deadweight (dwt)

This is the difference in tonnes between the light and loaded displacement but its commercial importance is that it represents the total weight a ship can carry which includes cargo, fuel, stores, freshwater and so on. A student may come across the initials DWAT standing for deadweight all told.

More importantly to those concerned with the ship commercially are the initials DWCC standing for deadweight cargo capacity. This indicates the potential earning capacity of a ship but it is not a figure that is cast in stone. When quoted in a ship's description it assumes that the maximum quantity of stores and bunkers are on board.

Loadlines

These are dictated by the International Loadline Convention of 1966 which is the basis of the current loadline system.

The amount of a ship's deadweight is determined by its loadline and this varies slightly because a ship has a maximum draught to which it is permitted to be loaded. This differs according to the part of the world in which the ship is loading and what season of the year. When reference is being made to a ship's deadweight without any qualification it invariably refers to the amount that can be loaded to its summer draught.

The ship's maximum draught and its variations are determined according to an internationally established formula. The International Loadline Convention of 1966 forms the basis of the current loadline calculation system, but it has a much older history. In 1876 Samuel Plimsoll a campaigning British politician succeeded in persuading the government of the day to pass a Merchant Shipping Act. This gave the authorities the power to detain unsafe ships and by an amendment drawn up in 1894 it particularly introduced a loadline. This was the deepest draft to which a ship could be loaded and was shown on the starboard side of the ship by a painted circular disc 12 inches in diameter with a line 18 inches long drawn horizontally through its centre to show the loadline. Because of Plimsoll's involvement, the loadline is sometimes referred to as a Plimsoll Mark.

The decision as to where the load line shall be situated is made at the time the ship is constructed and the decision process is overseen by the ship's Classification Society which issues the Load Line Certificate and supervises the placing of the loadline. This mark is situated approximately amidships on both sides of the vessel.

The freeboard of a ship is the distance from the upper deck to the loadline. Different parts of the world and different seasons are considered to vary in their degree of danger and so vary in the amount of freeboard necessary for safety. International convention has divided the world into zones the least dangerous of which is titled Tropical zone and the most dangerous is Winter, North Atlantic. Furthermore, saltwater provides more buoyancy to a ship than freshwater so that if the ship loads in freshwater it may be loaded to a deeper draft as she will rise up to the correct draft when reaching the ocean.

The ship

For these reasons a ship's loadline can have as many as six marks, each of which has an initial against it which represents:

TF = Tropical Zone, Fresh Water

F = Fresh Water

T = Tropical Zone (Salt water)

S = Summer (in other zones)

W = Winter (in other zones)

WNA = Winter North Atlantic

The actual mark (the disc with a line through it) is the Summer Mark. On the line are placed the initials of the Classification Society that surveyed the ship to determine the positioning of the mark. In the illustration is LR (Lloyd's Register) but there are several more such as AB (American Bureau) or RI (Registro Italiana) and so on.

Draught

This word, which can also be spelt draft, so far as this chapter is concerned refers to the distance between the bottom of the ship to the level of water on the ships side.

The more cargo (weight) the ship loads the deeper the ship will lay in the water and the greater its draught.

For some bulk cargoes, the taking of a draught reading before commencement of loading and then again when loading is finished gives a good check on the weight of cargo that has been loaded. This is called a draft survey and when it is of critical importance it is usually carried out either jointly by personnel from the ship and from the terminal or by an independent surveyor.

Ship Measurement based on Volume

There is another important reason for knowing the measurement of the interior of the ship. Some cargoes are far bulkier than they are heavy. Visualise the difference in the space that would be occupied by a tonne of feathers compared to a tonne of steel. It would be pointless arranging for a quantity of cargo equivalent to the ship's DWCC if there was simply insufficient room in which to stow it.

For this reason it is vital to know the stowage factor of the cargo This is the number of cubic metres or cubic feet to the tonne, and to know the cubic capacity of the ship. A ship always has two cubic capacities. One is referred to as the grain cubic which is the measurement of the total cargo space on the basis that materials like loose grain flow into all the spaces in the holds. The other figure, the smaller of the two, is the bale capacity that measures around rather than in and out of all the beams and girders in the hold. This, as the name implies, imagines the way bales of materials could not occupy the awkward corners.

Stowage

All cargoes have their own characteristic density which for the purpose of shipping is referred to as the stowage factor.

Although cubic capacities are now measured in cubic metres many shipbrokers all around the world still use cubic feet when quoting stowage factors. Partly this is because it is easier to work with and remember stowage factors when quoted in cubic feet. Wheat for example has a stowage factor between 40 and 44 cubic feet/tonne. The equivalent in metric would be 1.133 to 1.246 m^3/tonne.

Chapter 2

Chapter 3
Modern shipping and trade

Post-panamax container ship

Chapter 3

3.1 WHY TRADE GREW

Seaborne trade developed over the years as shippers experimented with more and more diverse types of cargo. Highly developed countries depended on their own natural resources to gain that position. Often this was at the expense of neglecting such industries as agriculture. Thus the import of foodstuffs increased.

But let us first concentrate upon the implications of distribution of resources. There are two concepts commonly used when considering the theory of trade. The first is absolute advantage, which refers to a commodity that one country has in exportable quantities but which another country has none or one country can produce the commodity cheaper than the other.

The second concept is comparative advantage. This concept comes into play when one of the countries is more efficient at producing goods. By allowing trade and specialising in the comparative advantage both countries have improved and trade is beneficial for both.

Some island countries such as Japan, with no natural resources, were forced to embrace an increase in all kinds of imports in order to expand and develop. Initially then, foodstuffs and raw materials such as ore and coal were shipped.

'Agnes Muir' built 1869 and traded to New Zealand.

In the reverse direction, export markets were identified and developed. Thus in the 19th century seaborne trade tended to comprise raw materials and agricultural products one way and manufactured goods the other. Cargo volumes in each direction were very much restricted by the sizes of the sailing vessels of the time. The arrival of steam ships changed things.

At the same time, the discovery of oil in both Baku and the USA saw kerosene lamps replace candles and the oil trade was born. At first oil was transported in barrels, then in square tins. This mode of transport gave way to dedicated ships called oil tankers. This saw the birth of a specialisation in ship design.

In the tanker sector there were some concerns that the introduction of electric lighting would scupper the tanker trade. But the development of the private motor car and commercial road transport saw this area of shipping prosper. The dawn of a new century would herald the rapid expanse of the maritime industry, the like of which had never been experienced before.

3.2 BULK SHIPPING GROWTH

Global industrialisation produced enormous demand for raw materials. Shipments of iron ore and other minerals essential for the production of specialist steels increased. Coking coal for steel-making and steam coal for electricity generation was widely traded.

Wheat, corn, barley, rice and soya beans was shipped in huge quantities. Livestock was shipped on the hoof. James Galbraith had pioneered the trade in chilled and frozen meat and thus another ship design was developed.

Millions of bales of cotton from Egypt and the USA was transported by sea as well as wool and flax. Industrial fibres such as Manila hemp and sisal for rope-making was shipped in from the Philippines and East Africa. Tea from India and Kenya, rubber from Malaya, coffee from Brazil, all were transported by the thousands of tonnes per month.

Countries with huge areas to cover embraced the railway system. This generated trade where steel rails, locomotives, carriages and goods wagons were imported. New ships sprouted heavy-lift derricks for loading and discharging these cargoes.

This posed the question, if railways, why not tugs barges and ferries; nothing was impossible as world trade expanded.

The Portsmouth-built battleship *HMS Dreadnought* saw steam turbines being pioneered for large ships. These gradually replaced steam-reciprocating engines in merchant ships, but these were, in turn, replaced by more economical marine diesel engines. These increased in output as the numbers of cylinders grew and increases in bores and strokes were seen.

Ship sizes increased and then reached a plateau as port facilities placed a constraint on any further expansion. This impasse continued in the dry cargo sector until the 1960s.

The Panama Canal slashed steaming times between the Atlantic and the Pacific.

Chapter 3

3.3 CRUDE OIL AND PRODUCTS

Tanker developments moved from cargoes of crude oil transported to oil refineries in consumer areas to a mixed market comprising both crude oils and refined products. Scientists discovered that oil was an extremely versatile raw material. This resulted in more products such as plastics, fertilisers and chemical gases being manufactured.

Tankers used the Suez Canal to shorten steaming distances from the Middle East to Europe and the USA.

Crude oil tankers were of a fairly simple design capable of carrying only two or three grades. On the other hand, clean tankers grew in sophistication as demands for a greater number of different grades were established.

World economic growth saw a widening in scope and size of clean tankers. Standard-design product carriers were sketched on naval architect's drawing boards in the 1960s.

3.4 GAS CARRIERS

In the 1960s a need was seen for hydrocarbon gas carriers. There were two varieties of gas to be transported. One was a product of the refining process and mainly comprised butane and propane, broadly classified as petroleum gases. The other was natural gas, a component of the crude oil production process. Each was handled in a different way.

Petroleum gas carriers were designed with a hull in which was a series of pressurised gas containers. Some carried the gas under pressure where it liquefied. Others had their cargoes semi-refrigerated which reduced the volume of the liquid. The final design was fully-refrigerated which reduced the volume of the cargo even more. The second and third varieties were insulated to a greater or lesser extent. But sufficient to get close to retaining loaded temperatures with a little assistance from on-board machinery.

Modern shipping and trade

LPG tanker 'Gaschem Jümme'

Natural gas, usually methane, was transported in a different manner. It was found that by lowering the temperature of the gas by a huge margin, the volume reduced accordingly. A temperature reduction to -165°C reduces the volume 500-fold. But of course carriage at that temperature requires heavy and efficient insulation. The ships were termed Liquefied Natural Gas (LNG) carriers.

The gas was liquefied at the loading terminal and this operation used roughly 12% of the cargo's energy to produce such low temperatures.

While no insulation material is totally efficient, the cargo was likely to warm slightly on passage. This change in temperature produced what was called cargo boil-off. It was captured at the tank top and used under the ship's boilers to produce steam for propulsion.

One of the original LNG carriers was the Vickers-Armstrong built *Methane Princess* of 27,400-cubic metres. It enjoyed a career of nearly 35 years. The beauty of these ships is that they discharge into a regasification plant from where the cargo, now at ambient temperature, can be pumped straight into the country's domestic gas pipeline grid.

Chapter 3

Original LNG carriers, Methane Princess and Methane Progress were built in 1964 to carry gas from Libya to Canvey Island in the River Thames.

3.5 DEVELOPMENT OF CONTAINERS

By the 1960s the plateau which restricted ship's sizes in the dry market was beginning to disappear. The loading and discharging of general cargo was seen as too labour-intensive and too time-consuming; ships were spending a week or ten days in port. The American haulier Malcolm McLean had developed a cargo container which could be lifted off a truck chassis in a laden condition and lifted onto a ship.

At the cargo's discharge port, the container was lifted off the ship and lowered onto a different lorry chassis and delivered to its final destination. The advantages of this system led to international rules governing the sizes and strengths of these containers being established.

Thereafter, new specialised container ship designs were produced, each one larger than the previous one. Due to of their high cost, shipping companies joined together in consortia to buy these new ships. Each one replaced two existing traditional ships in sheer size. Additionally their high speed and shorter berth occupancy multiplied this figure considerably.

Early Overseas Container Line (OCL) vessels carried some 1,900-teu. Their triple steam turbine propulsion and 28-knot service speed produced a fuel consumption of some 500 tonnes of fuel oil per day.

Later ships were larger and were fitted with marine diesel machinery which increased their economy while sacrificing only a few knots in speed. This was fortunate in that OPEC had increased the price of oil fourfold about the time that these ships were delivered.

As the container revolution spread, the days of the general cargo ship were numbered. Pioneers of the container trade such as the *Encounter Bay* have gradually been replaced by larger ships. Initially trade routes restricted sizes to what became known as Panamax size. These had a beam restricted by the 32.2m width of the Panama locks. This equated to 13 containers across the ship.

Modern shipping and trade

Early container ship.

A typical Panamax container ship has a capacity of about 5,000-teu. The expansion plans currently being put into place in the Panama Canal will see this size increase to about 12,500-teu in 2014. These are dubbed New-Panamax sizes. The largest ships in existence such as AP Moller's 'E'-class ships of about 14,700 are still post-New-Panamax, as are the 18,000-teu giants currently under construction.

The first steel was cut for the lead vessel in this class on the 14th May 2012. A series of 20 such vessels have been ordered by AP Moller from Daewoo Shipbuilding and Marine Engineering in South Korea.

Each will be 400m in length with a beam of 59m. The main deck is wide enough to accommodate four football pitches across the ship. The first is due for delivery in 2013.

Moller's new design of 18,000-teu container ship.

The new generation of container ship will have installed power of 88,500-bhp with two engines compared with 107,300 in the old e-class with just one diesel. This will give a service speed of 23-knots.

3.6 OFFSHORE

The discovery of oil in the North Sea in the Forties field in the 1960s spawned a worldwide spread of a completely new industry: The offshore industry and the associated offshore support vessels, (OSVs).

The first recognisable and dedicated OSV is generally considered to have been the *Ebb Tide*, built in 1956 to service the US Gulf offshore oil and gas industry. The US Gulf is where the OSV industry began and developed before spreading globally during the 1960s and 1970s.

The influences that subsequently affected OSV designs came from many different areas; principally fishing, towage and salvage, the barge industry and the heavy lift industry. The specific challenges of discharging and back-loading cargoes between an installation and a vessel, often in adverse weather conditions, have also determined the design standards.

In the early years, all of these influences created a vessel with more power than its size would normally warrant, with its accommodation and wheelhouse well forward and with a large clear wood-sheathed main deck aft of the accommodation block for the carriage of deck cargo. With two main engines, two shafts, twin propellers and bow thrusters, the emphasis was on manoeuvrability. Within the hull were cargo tanks for fuel, potable water, liquid mud and cement and a range of pumps was needed to discharge each of these cargoes.

Pioneering offshore supply ship Ebb Tide in the 1950s.

This is still the basic configuration of almost all OSVs sailing today, some 50 years later, although the size and complexity of the vessels has significantly increased.

The support requirements of the offshore oil and gas industry have developed continuously. The growth in the use of semi submersible drilling rigs produced a demand for specialist anchor handling vessels and for the development of drilling techniques produced a need to carry a wider variety of drilling fluids on PSVs.

Improvements in onshore logistics, as well as increased pipe laying capability, created a demand for larger platform supply vessels (PSVs), while the increase in subsea construction and inspection, repair and maintenance (IRM) operations drove the need for efficient ROV and diving support vessels and a host of other specialist ships.

Modern shipping and trade

While the US Gulf type OSVs were the first vessels to support the offshore oil and gas industry, it soon became clear that the harsher environmental conditions in several of the new regions being explored would require much larger, more powerful and more robust vessels to service their needs.

Tidewater's OSV *James Mclellan* in bad weather.

The transition was most obvious in the North Sea where, over a period of 15 years, the US Gulf type vessels were steadily replaced by the new breed of OSVs designed and built in Europe. In more environmentally benign regions, such as the Arabian Gulf and West Africa, this change has taken much longer and is driven by factors such as safety, increased cargo requirements, longer transit distances, increased reliability and redundancy and legislative demands.

The offshore industry uses a wide variety of vessel types that are specific to the roles associated with various stages of the exploration and production phases during an oil field's life cycle. While many of these vessels are single-role, an increasing number of them have been built with a multi-role capability to enhance their employment prospects. This not only makes the definitions of such vessels more complicated but it also introduces regulatory complications.

One example is the emergency response and rescue vessel (ERRV). These vessels are generally only used within the North Sea. Their role is to provide emergency cover for the platform or rig in the event of someone falling overboard or should the rig need to be evacuated quickly, before helicopters can arrive.

In addition to providing the rescue cover, these vessels can have functions such as fire-fighting, oil spill response, shuttle tanker mooring, protection of the installation's 500 metre exclusion zone, floating storage and related tasks.

3.7 BIG IS BETTER!

Since the start of the last century, shipping has expanded in leaps and bounds. As emphasised earlier, diversity has also grown.

Tanker sizes grew from just a few thousand tonnes deadweight to ships such as the Seawise Giant of 565,000-dwt.

Bulk carriers grew in size from 6,000-dwt to 400,000-dwt. Dry cargo ships increased in size from 8,000-dwt to containers ships under construction of 165,000-dwt.

New specialist vessels emerged. In the tanker sector, clean product tankers led to chemical tankers. Gas tankers emerged on the scene. High-heat asphalt and bitumen carriers were built as well as heavy scantling tankers designed for the carriage of caustic soda.

In the bulk carrier sector, new cargoes such as wood chips joined more traditional cargoes such as fertilisers, logs, timber, bauxite as well as dangerous cargoes like sulphur, direct reduced iron and nickel ore.

Passenger ferries grew in size and complexity. While passengers ships were replaced by airlines, the employment of these big floating palaces took on a cruising role.

'Oasis of the Seas' – 6,296 passengers and 2,394 crew.

So in the last century, the shipping industry has literally exploded in size. The paradox here is that it has slipped below the general public's radar.

Type of Ship	Numbers
Non-Passenger ships	
Tankers above 10,000-dwt	3,967
Tankers below 10,000-dwt	5,049
Chemical Tankers	3,680
Other Tankers	646
LPG Carriers	1,217
LNG Carriers	373
Bulk Carriers	8,890
Container Ships	5,093
Multi-purpose ships	3,053
General Cargo	15,329
Ro-Ro	2,263
Car Carriers	714
Refrigerated vessels	1,744
Offshore Support Vessels	5,207
Others	758
Total	**58,040**
Passenger Ships	
Mainline Passenger Ships & Cruise Liners	305
Expedition Ships	117
River Cruise Vessels	547
Passenger Ferries	792
Passenger Barges	79
Non-Expedition Cruise ships/Others	75
Total	**1,915**
Grand Total	**59,995 vessels**

Number of vessels in service. (From 2012 Clarkson's figures and other industry sources.)

Chapter 3

Chapter 4
The port

Tanker berth

Chapter 4

4.1 INTRODUCTION

A port is a safe and secure place for ships to load and unload freight and passengers. Its infrastructure will have been designed or will have evolved for this purpose and the emphasis is on safety. The port must be as secure as possible from the wind and weather, the ship from hull and bottom damage and cargoes secure from theft or tampering.

Within a place of safety the commercial business of loading, unloading and replenishment of the ship is carried out. It can be performed either alongside a quay, at a buoy or at an anchorage, using barges and tenders.

Hong Kong harbour.

The key requirement for the location of a port is the commercial demand for the movement of goods and people. It does not follow that a safe place will be a port, but a port must be a safe place. Ports have developed in locations where there is natural safety, but today if required, safe harbours can be constructed.

4.2 GETTING CARGOES AFLOAT

To the shipper or passenger, a port is the interface between land and water transport. Its services will have been developed and fine-tuned to the developing requirements of the shipper. Good land transport links are required, as are facilities for storing and handling goods and processing passengers. These will have been updated over the years as circumstances dictated. Port costs are kept as low as possible to encourage trade and stimulate port growth.

4.3 GATEWAY

To the national economist, a port is a gateway to all the benefits of international trade. For this reason, governments will support and even subsidise their most important ports. Ports must be provided with both road and rail links to deliver cargoes to the port and to disperse incoming cargoes to the country.

The port

Ports must have good road and rail links.

4.4 INFRASTRUCTURE

Increasingly ports specialise in certain cargoes. In previous times, when ships varied little in size, ports tended to cater for every type from cargo and ships were berthed at the appropriate dock for their shipments. With economies of scale forcing an increase in ship sizes, new ports had to be built. It made sense to specialise so that some ports were designated as bulk mineral or grain berths while others were perhaps designed as container ports.

Port Hedland, Western Australia, specialises in the export of iron ore.

In the container sector the port forms part of the multimodal chain. This logistics procession starts with the stuffing of a container at a warehouse far removed from the port. A truck or train brings the container to the collecting yard at the docks. The container will then be loaded onto the ship. If it is a small feeder ship, it will proceed to a container hub such as Bremerhaven, Algeciras or Singapore. If it is a large ship, the port may well be the hub itself.

4.5 SPECIAL PORTS

A student of the shipping industry may well ask how a port works. It might be seen as a crossroads where a major road and a minor road meet. One road is used by cargo and the other by shipping. It is at this junction where it all happens.

Ports have different levels of complexity. A simple port is one like Abbot Point in Queensland, Australia. Its only reason for being there is to export coal.

Abbot Point terminal exports coal.

Metallurgical coal and thermal coal is exported from Abbot Point. It is shipped into the area by rail from mines at Newlands, Colinsville and from the Central Bowen Basin. Abbot Point was selected as a suitable place for a terminal as it was an area where deep water existed close to the shore. The ships berth across the end of a T-shaped jetty one and a half nautical miles off the coast. The water depth alongside is 21.5 metres.

The port has open areas close to the shoreline where coal handling facilities and stockpile areas are situated. Thus if we freeze everything there, the terminal is ready for business. An interesting question might be what happens next.

4.5.1 Case Study: Abbot Point

There has to be customer to buy a cargo of coal. From Abbot Point, coal is exported mainly to Japan which takes a large share of both grades of coal. South Korea and Taiwan take a large volume of thermal coal while India and China are large buyers of metallurgical coal. Our customer therefore is likely to be Japanese company.

It contacts the coal mining company and negotiate the purchase of 165,000 tonnes of coal to be delivered to South Japan in the middle of July. The mining company already has a sufficient stockpile of coal at Abbot Point to satisfy their customer's demand. The sea voyage from North Queensland to South Japan is 10-12 days steaming. The customer contacts the port authority to investigate whether there will be a berth available at the beginning of July.

Receiving a satisfactory response, the mining company asks its shipbroker to find a Capesize bulk carrier capable of loading 165,000 tonnes of coal at the beginning of July. The broker offers a selection of vessels and the mining company, or charterer, agrees a charter with an owner at for example, $10 per tonne.

International Shipbroker, Gibsons

The charterer issues voyage instructions to the shipowner which passes them to the ship's Master. Included in these orders will be an instruction to give seven days notice of arrival to the Abbot Point port authority. This is to be followed by three days notice, 48 hours, 24 hours and 12 hours notice. The Master will also have to follow the Australian reporting systems and replace the ships ballast water in mid-ocean to avoid bringing alien species into the country.

The charterer approaches the Port Authority and nominates the ship to them giving its name, size, flag, an approximate arrival date and cargo destination. The charterer will already have an agent in the port and this information is shared with the ship agency.

Chapter 4

The agent will alert the pilot and the tug company to expect the arrival of the ship as well as the linemen who will take the ship's mooring lines. They alert the customs and immigration service, advising them of the bulker's itinerary. They issue a pro-forma disbursement account which details the port charges the shipowner will have to bear. These will include port costs, pilotage, tug and linesmen costs, agency fees and any other charges. They will ask the shipowner to put them in funds.

As the ship approaches the port, a pilot will board. They will guide the vessel alongside the berth with the aid of attending tugs. The linemen will take the ship's mooring lines and the crew will berth the ship snugly alongside the berth. The ship will be deballasting and the crew sliding open the hatches ready to receive the cargo.

The customs and immigration will board the ship to ensure that there are no infringements to Australia's laws and that all legal obligations are being observed. The agent will board the ship to conclude all the usual formalities and make sure all the Master's requirements are met.

Coal berth for large bulk carriers.

The operators and the loading gangs will manoeuvre the coal loader over the hatches. The bucket loader will take bite after bite of coal from the stockpile area. The giant conveyor belts will trundle the coal the nearly three kilometres distance out to the ship loader and loading will commence.

In Australia, loading is progressed at about, 4,600 tonnes per hour. Thus a cargo of 165,000 tonnes takes less than two days to load. The ship's agent will tell the Harbour Master when the ship is due to complete. Tugs and linemen and the pilot will be ordered and the customs and immigration officials will be kept informed of progress.

During loading the ship's officers will ensure that the cargo is being stowed correctly. It will need to be evenly shared among the nine holds to prevent any needless stresses to the ship's hull. On completion of loading, the duty officer will record the draught marks painted on the hull. From these figures an approximate check can be made on the cargo amount loaded; the larger the quantity, the deeper the ship will be submersed.

The port

Draught marks indicating how deep the ship has been submerged by weight of cargo.

The port authority will have a system in place to accurately measure the quantity of coal passing along its conveyor belts.

When the final amount of cargo has been established, the agent will draw up Bills of Lading and Mate's Receipts to be signed by the Master and a cargo manifest drawn up. The vessel will be issued with customs and port clearance and be given the green light to sail.

The crew will have closed and battened down the hatches. The pilot will board, the tugs will pass their towing wires to be made fast to the ship. The linemen will be in position to let go the ship's mooring lines.

The pilot checks with the Master that he is in agreement with the proceedings.

With the affirmation, the pilot will instruct the lines to be let go, the tugs to pull, the engine to start and the vessel's laden voyage begins.

Back ashore, trains will continue to empty their coal into the storage area. There will a collective sigh of relief that another ship has safely loaded and sailed. The next ship will be awaited.

Abbot Point handles about 1.2m tonnes of coal per month. That is the equivalent of one Capesize vessel arriving every four days. There are plans for an expansion to 50m tonnes per annum.

4.5.2 Case Study: Richards Bay

Other ports are not just single-trade facilities. One could look at Richards Bay as an example.

Richards Bay in Kwazulu Natal is highly flexible for both imports and exports.

An aerial view of the port shows how many different facilities are available. The port is famous in international shipping for its coal exports. Its six berths and four ship loaders enable the port to export 91m tonnes per year. As such it is the largest coal export terminal in the world. The largest ship to use the port is the 372,201-det Brazilian Pride, which had a length of 363.7m, a beam of 63.4m and a maximum draught of 21.8m.

Additionally it has other attractions. Its good railway links makes it attractive for timber, woodchip and granite exports from the Eastern Cape and taking trade away from Durban.

In the last year it has handled the following bewildering array of cargoes: Andalusite, Chrome, Magnetite, Ferro Fines, Fertiliser products, Rock Phosphate, Rutile, Titanium Slag, Vanadium Slag, Vermiculite, Woodchips, Zircon, Alumina, Coking Coal, Anthracite, Manganese, Petcoke, Rock Phosphate, Salt and Sulphur.

Handysize bulk carrier 'Antonia'

In 2010 Richards Bay handled close to 85m tonnes of cargo. Not bad for a port of which Commissioner Henry Cloete was so dismissive in 1843. He surveyed the Mhlatuge estuary and expressed the opinion that it had little or no potential as a harbour.

4.6　MULTI CARGO PORTS

4.6.1　Rotterdam

Another port which had an unpromising outlook from an early stage must have been Rotterdam. It is one of the many exits that the River Rhine makes into the North Sea. The source of the Rhine is near the town of Andermatt in the south of Switzerland where in spring and summer it is fed by snow melt from the mountainous Swiss interior.

It picks up more water from some 14 tributaries from one side and 25 from the other bank along the way. It drains much of south Germany on its way to the sea. Due to its size it enters the North Sea via a huge delta system, the largest in Europe.

Deltas are areas predisposed to silting, shifting sandbanks and meandering channels, all of which change when the river is in full spate. The extremely high tides which the area experiences add to the turmoil. A tidal range of about seven metres is common in the Dover Strait and the southern North Sea. Thus even buildings built on a river bank might be expected to have an uncertain future.

But the Dutch are experts at taming the elements, especially when it comes to water. No one builds water channels, conduits, canals and dikes like the Dutch. Much of the coastal reaches of the Netherlands lay below sea level. This was not seen as an obstacle. The simple plan was to build a wall across the entrances to wide bays and empty the enclosed water out, replacing it with dredged soil from outside the enclosure; a seemingly easy solution. That was the fate of the Zuiderzee.

Making Amsterdam and Rotterdam workable ports was childs play. To expand them to the size they are today, even easier. Rotterdam's main channel has been dredged to more than 20 metres. It can take the largest ships in the world. Its container cranes have an outreach to service the beamiest of post-new-panamax boxships. Europe with all its giant ports all part of a multi-headed gorgon-like arrangement all gagging for cargoes like chicks in a nest; Rotterdam would have the largest mouth. Its imports come from all over the globe. Its exports come in from all over Europe, by barge, by rail, by road and by feeder ship. From uncertain beginnings, the Dutch have triumphed: It might in future be considered to be a wonder of the world.

4.6.2 Suez Canal

Other triumphs in the maritime world involve the digging of ditches to act as short cuts. They started as smallish projects. The Avon-Kennet canal joined Bristol with London but such small ventures were overtaken by an expanding railway network.

There were larger projects in prospect. In the 18th and first half of the 19th centuries, voyages from Europe to the Far East necessitated a trip around the southern tip of Africa or the even longer mission around Cape Horn. The eyes of the shipping developers alighted on Egypt. What about a canal between the Mediterranean and the Gulf of Suez? Thus the idea for the Suez Canal was born.

It took 10 years to build and over this period it was thought that over a million construction workers were involved. It opened in November 1869 with the yacht *Aigle* being the first to transit the canal followed by the P&O passenger liner, *Delta*. Fortunately sea levels are similar between the Red Sea and the Mediterranean so there is no discernible current.

It had an original depth of eight metres. Over the years it has been deepened and widened so that now it has a depth of 24m and a width of 205m. Ships go through in convoys with two passing places. A southbound convoy stops in the Great Bitter Lake while the northbound convoy passes. The southbound convoy ups anchor and heads south again while the northbound convoy waits at El Quantara for the next southbound convoy to pass.

And when you stand on a ship's bridge looking down the straight length of the canal, the water and the two banks conspire to emphasise the curvature of the earth as they disappear over the horizon. There are few places on earth where it is quite so dramatic.

4.6.3 Panama Canal

Another dramatic construction project was the Panama Canal. The USA long-planned a short-cut between the Atlantic and the Pacific. It was started in 1880 but was not completed until 1914. The drama of working in the mosquito swamps has been well documented. Suffice it to say that more than 22,000 workers died from accidents, malaria and yellow fever.

The transit distance is only 48 miles. But with the Miraflores series of locks one end and the Gatun locks at the other, the transit takes about a day. Ships are lifted up and dropped by the locks nearly 60 feet to climb over the central spine of the isthmus. The traditional beam of 32.2 metres in the locks has influenced ship designs for decades.

The establishment of the canal has been beneficial to the US Navy. It has reduced the need to have a large Pacific fleet and an equally large Atlantic fleet. Its major fleet units have been designed with the canal dimension very much to the fore.

The canal is now being enlarged so that the dimensions will provide a facility to handle ships with a beam increased from 32.2m to 49m. The length restriction will be increased from 282m to 366m. The opening ceremony is planned for 2014. The total cost of $5.25bn is high but compared with the cost of the largest of the US Navy nuclear aircraft carriers, it is quite low. The latest Gerald R. Ford-class of supercarrier will cost $14bn and while being too large to transit the current canal will be able to transit the enlarged one. The new class is due for delivery in 2014; which incidentally is the same date that the new canal opens.

The enlarged canal will be beneficial to container lines in their round-the world services. They are currently restricted to Panamax-type vessels of about 5,000-teu. Increased canal dimensions will allow vessels of 9,500-teu.

Chapter 4

Chapter 5
Essential ingredients for the shipping cake

Floating crane

Chapter 5

5.1 TRADITIONAL SHIP-OWNER

A traditional ship-owner was one which saw an opportunity and built and operated ships to fill that vacuum. The chemical company Lever Brothers had palm tree plantations in West Africa and the Solomon Islands. Palm Line was established to bring in bulk vegetable oil to the Unilever soap-making factories in the UK.

James Galbraith experimented with refrigeration machinery that enabled frozen and chilled meat to be brought to the UK from Australia and New Zealand. With colleagues he set up what became Shaw Savill and Albion. Seeing a similar opportunity in South America, the Houlder brothers started a similar trade with Argentina.

These became niche markets, but international shipping has now explored all possible niches and it is thought that no more are possible.

5.2 MODERN SHIP-OWNER

In essence there are two styles of ship-owner in the modern era. There are those companies that play with all their cards on the table. In this area, everything is transparent; income, profit, tax, dividends, investments, shareholders, charter hire rates and any future plans.

In stark contrast there are those ship-owners who work in a very secretive way. Their ships are owned by one-ship companies, signified by a brass plaque on the wall of some obscure office block in the Cayman Islands. The ships are operated by a ship management company. The vessels are manned by a crewing company in the Philippines. The ships are registered in the Marshall Islands or Panama. The owner is not obliged to publish any company reports and accounts. And more important of all from the owners' point of view, they pay no tax.

This has little effect when markets are high; this century, large bulk carriers have earned as much as $250,000 per day. A 75-day round voyage from Brazil to China would provide an income of some $18m with voyage costs of little more than $2m. In such circumstances, opinions about flags of convenience are somewhat muted. But when the market down-turn comes as it always does, these concerns become more pronounced, but the market has always been one of supply and demand. Some demand is always there, but the tonnage supply always has a regulating effect.

5.3 GET A SHIP

Apart from the liner trade, the employment of a ship always comes with a variety of calls, but the main thrust of the demand is 'get me a ship'. This is usually directed at a shipbroker by merchants. They may have a cargo of iron ore or coal, or it could be crude oil or gasoline, or logs or grain; the variety of bulk cargoes is endless.

But the requirement for a ship is always present: Not only the type of ship is an issue, but whether it is fit for purpose. This is where ship inspection databases come into their own. Systems such as EQUASIS will tell all concerned whether the ships are suitable for a particular trade. The shipbroker has the experience to know at a glance which ship will fit the charterer's requirements.

Brokers keep long lists of where ships are and when they could reach various loading ports. Generally speaking cargoes are quoted on a private basis. The merchant calls his brokers and tells them the size of the cargo, what the cargo is, where it is loading, where it is discharging and the loading dates.

- **Cargo** - this could be coal, iron ore, other mineral ores, grain, steels, scrap, timber, logs, woodchips and suchlike for dry cargo. For tankers, it could be crude oil, dirty refined products, clean refined products, chemicals, bitumen, asphalt or gas varieties.
- **Cargo size** – This would be quoted in tonnes or sometimes in the case of oil, barrels. There again, there could be a cargo quoted in cubic metres.

Essential ingredients for the shipping cake

- **Loading area or port** – This is normally be an area such as UK Continent (Gibraltar-Hamburg range). Or it could be a port such as Richards Bay or Seven Islands. There will also be an option for one or two berths or one or two ports.
- **Discharging area or port** – The same applies for the discharge port or area. It could be Far East (Singapore-Japan range). It might be US Atlantic Coast or US Gulf.
- **Dates** – This is the loading date or the loading window. In the tanker trades it is usually a single day. In the dry cargo sector it could be a week or ten days.
- **Physical restrictions** – At the loading or discharging ports, there might be a draught restriction or a length limit at the berth. There might be bridge which ships might hit unless the air-draught is small enough.

With 58,000 ships trading in the world, it should be obvious that the numbers of shipping contracts or charters concluded every day may number in their hundreds rather than scores. Thus the shipping market is an exciting place to be close to.

5.4 CLASSIFICATION SOCIETIES

There are 13 main organisations. The best known is Lloyd's Register. The term 100A1 has entered the English language as a description of something which is of high quality.

International Association of Classification Societies (IACS)
The members of IACS are:

American Bureau of Shipping (ABS)	USA
Bureau Veritas (BV)	France
China Classification Society (CCS)	China
Croatian Register of Shipping (CRS)	Croatia
Det Norske Veritas (DNV)	Norway
Germanischer Lloyd (GL)	Germany
Indian Register of Shipping (IRS)	India
Korean Register of Shipping (KR)	South Korea
Lloyd's Register (LR)	UK
Nippon Kaiji Kyokai NK/Class NK	Japan
Polish Register of Shipping (PRS)	Poland
Registro Italiano Navale (RINA)	Italy
Russian maritime Register of Shipping (RS)	Russia

Ships are built to designs which have been approved by classification societies. During the building phase, Class surveyors are in attendance to ensure that the construction rules are being obeyed. The vessels are delivered to their owners with a class notation. This is renewed at the ship's special survey which usually takes place every five years. Vessels are compelled to undertake a special survey every four years, but if they have a history of continuous classification surveys, a year of grace is given.

ccasionally a vessel is withdran from one classification society and entered into another. However, there are many hoops to jump through in the process.

Chapter 5

Busy port

Port of Dover

5.5 NAVAL ARCHITECT

Before a ship is built, it has to be on the drawing board. In fact nowadays ships are designed on a computer with specialised software. All this work is done by a naval architect, either at the shipyard or by one employed by the owner of the ship. Once the plans are approved by a classification society, they are used by the shipyard to build the ship.

Naval architects are highly trained. There are specialised university degree courses at places such as Newcastle-upon-Tyne, Strathclyde or Southampton in the UK. These are three years courses in England and four in Scotland. In the USA there is only a handful of colleges that offer degree courses. These include Michigan, Iowa, South Florida and New England. Designing a small barge would be quite simple. But one's imagination would run wild if one considers the hurdles to be surmounted in designing a class1 passenger ships with their miles of cabling and piping serving thousands of cabins.

5.6 SHIPBUILDERS

Ships are built in modules which are then transported by gantry and crane to a building dock where they are welded together. When the vessel is ready, the building dock is flooded and the ship is towed out for the finishing touches to be made. Sea-trials are then carried out and if satisfactory, the ship is handed over to the owner.

There are numerous shipyards throughout the world. The hub concentrating on the mass production of ships moved from Europe to the Far East many years ago. Initially it moved to Japan, mainly on terms of cost. Then as Japanese-built ships became more expensive, the focus for such ships moved to South Korea. The Koreans had been accused of building ships at below cost to establish a competitive advantage. This was strenuously denied. But what goes around comes around and it became the South Koreans to cry foul as China took over as the largest shipbuilding country in the world. They claimed that Chinese pricing amounted to dumping.

But in recent years, ship-owners were seduced by cheap prices and the rush to order ships in China became a stampede. When the world recession set in, many of these ships became unwanted and many ship-owners have decided to forfeit the 30% deposit to get out of various deals. The vessels would have been delivered into a poor market where profits would have been difficult to find.

5.7 SHIP EQUIPMENT MANUFACTURERS

There is more to a ship than just a basic hull. It has to have an engine to propel it. The engine turns a shaft on which is a propeller. The ship must have electric power from diesel alternators to run its auxiliaries. The ship must have electric pumps to handle fuel, engine cooling water, water ballast and domestic fresh water. It must have a sewage plant for the crew as well as fully fitted out accommodation. Each officer and crew member has a cabin with en-suite bathroom facilities.

The crew must be fed, so the ship has a galley with store rooms and refrigerator rooms. The ship must be able to handle cargo. This is by pump if it is a liquid cargo or by crane if it loads and discharges dry cargo. Larger ships tend to e loaded and discharged by shore equipment, but nevertheless the ship usually has holds or tanks which have to have a means of being opened and closed.

Chapter 5

Ships need ropes and wires to moor up.

Navigation equipment such as compasses, radar, satellite navigation and steering gear also has to be supplied. All this equipment has to be bought in from suppliers around the world to enable the ship to be properly fitted out. And since the sea is a very unforgiving environment, all the equipment has to be top quality.

In the days of wooden ships, the gaps between the planks were sealed or caulked with cotton and hot tar. This made the ship watertight. From this came the proverb, *don't spoil the ship for a ha'p'orth of tar*. In a wider sense, it means don't jeopardise an enterprise by scrimping on small things. This is still relevant in the shipbuilding industry today.

5.8 PORT WORKERS

A ship is not a standalone object though. Apart from the officers and crew which operate it, it needs shore support. To enable the ship to go in and out of port, it requires a pilot to guide it through the channels. It needs tugs to manoeuvre it. It needs linemen to make it fast alongside. It requires shore labour to load and discharge it before it can get on its way again.

Pilots are transported from the shore to the ship by pilot boat although in some cases a helicopter is used. There pilot boats with good sea-keeping qualities are required and they require crews. Then there are the pilots themselves who are invariably ex-seafarers.

Tugs are normally used to escort ships into ports and to assist in the berthing process. These need tug skippers and crews. Linemen take the heavy ropes and wires and place them over bollards and mooring hooks. Customs and immigration personnel conduct the port and country's business according to local laws and regulations.

There are cargo workers and tally clerks that ensure the right cargo goes into the right space on the ship. Or they ensure the correct cargo is discharged. There is a whole security industry involved in keeping ships and port premises safe.

Essential ingredients for the shipping cake

Ships take on stores and water in most ports and thus there must be these support services available. Often bunker fuel is taken on board. In the cse of tankers, this can be loaded from shore lines. In most other places a bunker barge or small tank ship goes alongside the ship and pumps oil onboard.

Bunkers are supplied in most ports.

Chapter 5

5.9 SHIPS AGENTS

Ship-owners cannot have an office in each port to handle ship's business. They therefore appoint an agent to represent them and to make sure that all the ship's requirements are attended to. The vessel might require fuel or water. It may need stores or spare parts; it will definitely need someone with local knowledge to deal with the cargo receivers and officials such as customs and immigration. A big tanker or bulk carrier's operating costs can be cloe to $10,000 per day; much more if one adds the financing costs into the equation. Therefore every hour or every day saved equals a large sum of money.

Container cranes destined for Rotterdam.

5.10 CARGO HANDLING

The handling of a ship's cargo used to be extremely labour-intensive. Now it is very machinery dependent. Shore cranes, shiploaders and unloaders are all employed to put cargo into a ship or to take it out. In the case of a container ship, container cranes handle hundreds of containers every day. Straddle carriers and fork lift truks manoeuvre the containers around the stacking areas. Trucks and trains service the port area delivering and taking containers away from the port area.

Essential ingredients for the shipping cake

Insurers and PandI clubs are essential.

Bulk cargoes such as coal, iron ore and grain are generally carried to and from the ship by conveyor belt. They are loaded through chutes and discharged by suction or grabs. The design and manufacture of cargo handling equipment is a huge industry in itself.

5.11 INSURERS

Safety is always a top priority in the shipping industry, but accidents can happen. This is where insurers or underwriters enter the picture. Generally speaking a ship-owner pays a premium to an insurer and in return the ship's hull and machinery is insured against all risks. Simplistically speaking if the ship sinks, the insured value of the ship is paid to the owner. Lloyd's is the best known insurance market and risks are covered by a consortium called a syndicate.

5.12 PROTECTION AND INDEMNITY CLUB (P&I CLUB)

There are several types of Club, although by far the largest and financially strongest sector are Ship-owners' Protection and Indemnity Associations, mutual and non-profit making organisations which provide insurance cover fr ship-owners and operators which is complementary to the insurance cover placed on the insurance market, and which was discussed briefly in Chapter 8.

Chapter 5

Insurers and PandI clubs are essential.

There is no precise dividing line between the cover afforded by insurance companies and that provided by P&I Clubs. In fact PandI insurance is also available to a limited degree from the insurance market While Clubs traditionally provide one quarter of a shipowner's collision insurance liability, in general terms it might be said that Lloyd's underwriters and insurance companies insure ships and cargoes, whilst ship-owners P&I Clubs insure their liabilities.

For the most part, P&I clubs are mutual associations where the members are both the insured and the insurer. This means that the members must each contribute to a level sufficient to ensure that all claims against all members can be satisfied. Clubs are run on a non-profit basis. There are also some commercial companies that offer P&I cover on a fixed premium basis.

Two of the factors which contributed to the formation of Shipowner's P&I Clubs were the additional risks which shipowners had to assume following the almost universal acceptance of the Hague Rules, and for British ships, the reluctance of underwriters to accept more than three-quarters of an owner's liability for damage done to another ship in a collision. In other parts of the world, there has not been this reluctance and so the P&I clubs in those areas – Scandinavia is a good example – do not offer the extra hull insurance as it is not needed. Accordingly owners associated together on a mutual basis, forming the directing boards of the Clubs, whose managers are mostly professional legal partnerships with legal experience. Subscriptions (or 'calls') are made annually based on the tonnage entered and on the record of the party involved. A high claims record should mean that the calls will be levied at a higher rate than for an entered owner with a low claims record. If forecasted claims are higher than expected, supplementary calls will need to be levied to enable the Club to pay its way.

'Protection' would deal with matters such as: one quarter of owner's collision liability, personal injury, crew liabilities, damage to piers and the removal of wrecks.

'Indemnity' would involve: loss of or damage to cargo, a ship's proportion of General Average and customs' fines.

A third section of cover: 'Freight, Demurrage and Defence', would be concerned with the enforcement of legal proceedings for collection of freight and hire; conduct of actions and arbitrations and general legal advice to members.

5.13 MARINE SURVEYORS

Dry dock.

In many countries, road vehicles have to undergo an annual test for roadworthiness. A similar scheme is in place for all merchant ships. They are surveyed every year for seaworthiness. This is usually done on a continuous basis where certain aspects of the ship's makeup are chcked as it trades around the world. At the end of each year, the vessel will have undergone a thorough examination and the 'survey passed' box is ticked.

Chapter 5

Floating dry dock.

Such inspections get more rigorous each year until, at the end of each four-year period, an extra-stringent survey, if passed, gives the ship a year of grace before what is termed its special survey or SS has to be performed. The SS involves the ship being taken out of service and placed in a dry-dock where all the ship's equipment is checked or overhauled. It then gets a clean bill of health, its certificates are renewed and the whole process starts all over again.

These cycles are overseen and conducted my marine surveyors. These professionals are employed by classification societies and are expets at detecting faults and suggesting remedies. They crawl through all the unseen and forgotten spaces on board to ensure that a ship remains seaworthy.

Chapter 6
Ship Management

Shipping people

Chapter 6

6.1 SHIP MANAGEMENT

All ships need to be managed. The Masters needs to know where they are going and they need officers and crew to help them get there. The ship requires fuel and stores to perform its employment. It needs to be insured and all risks covered. There is a myriad of detail that needs to be attended to in order that any voyage is a success.

Before the age of wireless, Masters were very much left to their own devices to perform voyages. They arrived back in their home ports months or even years later having had little input from the head office.

But this is now a modern world and ship-owners and charterers demand to be kept informed of every detail of the voyage. But with this demand comes responsibility. With it comes the expectation from the ship that instructions guiding the whole voyage will be sent. In addition any small difficulty which is out of the ordinary will be addressed by head office.

6.2 THIRD-PARTY MANAGEMENT

Some shipping companies have their own management team which works from head office and sometimes from satellite offices. Others employ third-party management. This strategy depends upon economy of scale. An owner may manage its own ships but have spare capacity to manage other vessels as well. It then establishes an operation which will manage any number of ships as if they were its own.

The shipowner which has its ships managed by outside contractors pays a fee plus costs. This is seen as a cheaper alternative than employing shore staff itself to ship-manage. But there are various degrees of management.

6.3 CREW MANAGEMENT

As the name implies, this involves sourcing and supplying qualified officers and crews for a ship. Sea staff are contracted to work for a certain number of months and to have a certain number of month's shore leave. The ship manager needs to keep tabs on the ship's position so that crew changes may be made in a timely manner.

Large crew management companies have special arrangements with airlines or charter companies to fly large numbers of sea staff around the world.

Ideally these changes are staggered so that there is always a number of personnel on board who know how the particular vessel works. It would be dangerous to conduct a complete crew change so that not one of the new crew members knew any details of where equipment was, how things worked and have knowledge of all the little idiosyncrasies which a ship may have. Even sister ships may be similar but not identical.

The crew manager also arranges for crew wages to be paid and for families back home to be given sums requested by seafarers. These are commonly known as 'allotments'.

Crew change.

6.4 TECHNICAL MANAGEMENT

This type of management involves maintaining the physical wellbeing of a ship. Vessels have certificates to prove that it is seaworthy. The technical manager has to ensure that these are kept up to date. All ship surveys must be arranged and carried out. Any new pieces of equipment that the vessel is required to have either through legislation or under instruction from the owner must be sourced, dispatched and fitted.

Repairs, either planned or unforeseen must be arranged. Chart corrections and navigational equipment upgrades must be organised. The technical manager must ensure that the vessel can physically perform its lawful employment.

6.5 COMMERCIAL MANAGEMENT

This type of management is all to do with earnings. The commercial manager must ensure that the vessel can earn as much money as is possible given the state of the market in which it is trading. The commercial management team arranges charters for tankers and dry cargo ships. It attempts to maximise the time the vessel is performing laden passages and minimise the time it is travelling in ballast. It must seek the cheapest deal on pilotage and tugs and analyse the ship's performance.

Before a ship embarks upon a period of employment, a voyage calculation or voyage estimate is made. The bottom line of this calculation shows in dollars per day the amount the ship will earn after voyage expenses are deducted. This calculation is compared with other employment opportunities and the most profitable and practical option is undertaken.

All elements must be taken into account when making a commercial decision. It is no good sending a ship on a poorly-paid voyage where there is little opportunity of achieving a reasonable backhaul trip. All voyage calculations are made on a round-voyage basis. Thus any future employment that reduces the ballast leg can be taken as a bonus.

On completion of every voyage, the voyage estimate must be compared with the actual costs experienced and lessons on port costs, fuel charges, taxes, loading and discharging times, port delays and sundry other expenses realized, learnt.

Successful commercial management whether undertaken in-house, or placed with a third-party, is probably the most important element of a ship's administration.

Chapter 6

Chapter 7
Back office support

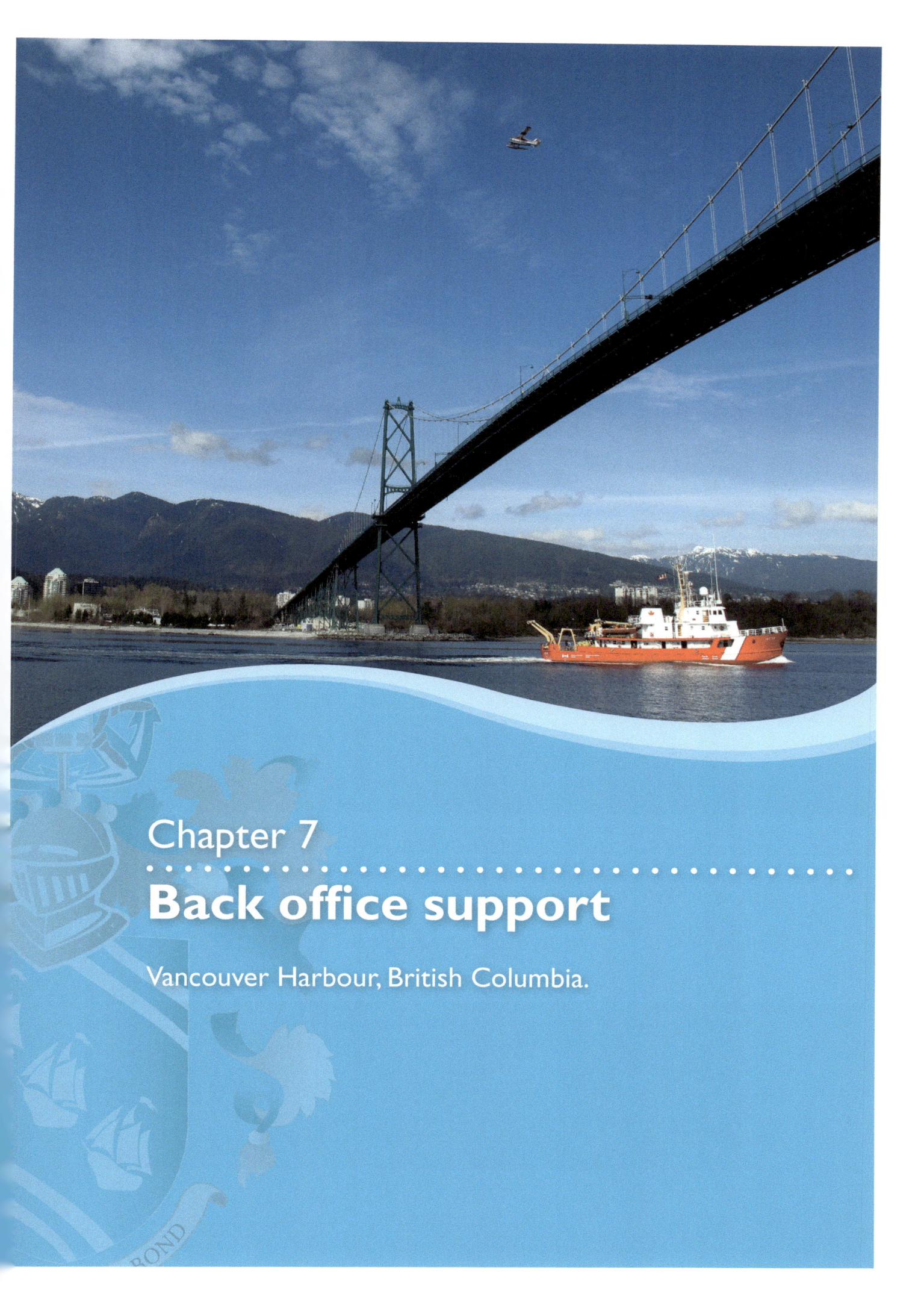

Vancouver Harbour, British Columbia.

Chapter 7

7.1 SHIPBROKERS

Shipbroking is a profession where its members gather and provide commercial information to ship-owners and to merchants. These are the shipbrokers' principals and it is to them that they look to for rewards for such a service.

Baltic Exchange, London.

Back office support

Shipbroking nowadays is invariably conducted on the telephone, assisted by electronic means of communication. It involves market information gathering and market analysis. It includes the dissemination of information to principals such that they obtain the best possible picture of the employment prospects for their ships if the owner. It provides the best possible view of the prospects of successfully chartering a ship, if the merchant or charterer.

Shipbrokers obtain firm offers from owners and pass them to the cargo principal in an effort to trigger negotiations which will lead eventually to a transportation contract or fixture.

The broker also provides an operational service such as the forwarding of voyage instructions, passing of information to both parties on the progress of the voyage and the transmission of a freight or hire invoice to the charterer.

On the conclusion of the voyage or trip, the broker will continue to be active in following up any demurrage or despatch claims or endeavouring to settle any disputes which might have arisen during the currency of the charter.

For this service, the broker is paid a commission, usually based on a percentage of the amount of freight or hire the vessel has earned.

Shipbrokers are also involved in the sale and purchase of ships, locating willing sellers and willing buyers of second-hand or new vessels.

These subjects are all covered in the ICS Dry Cargo Chartering, Tanker Chartering and Ship Sale and Purchase books.

7.2 BUNKER SUPPLIERS

Invariably a sea-going vessel requires fuel to propel it. Generally speaking there are two types. The first is fuel oil. This a residual oil, being the residue that remains after the rest of the refined products are removed. There are three usual grades, described by their viscosities. 350 centistokes (cst) is the heaviest fuel oil while 180 cst is an intermediate grade. 600 cst is a lighter grade used in smaller engines. There is a global limit to the sulphur content in fuel oils which is capped at 3.5%. In coastal areas the cap is 1%.

In the future, under IMO pollution regulations, the cap will be lowered to 0.1% sulphur content. It is not economically viable to reduce the sulphur content below 1% in fuel oil, so eventually ship's fuel oil will either have to be replaced by distillate fuels such as marine diesel oil or the ship's exhaust emissions will have to be scrubbed.

The second type of fuel is marine diesel oil, as mentioned above, a distillate fuel. Currently this fuel is used by small coastal ships, tugs and offshore support vessels for all propulsion and electricity generation purposes. It is also used in larger ships for slow speed and manoeuvring operations and in port.

The generic term for all marine oils is bunker fuel. These are supplied to ships in most ports in the world. And the further a ship is from a refinery port, the more expensive and the more difficult bunkers will be to obtain.

After planning the ship's programme, the owner, ship manager or operator will calculate the vessel's fuel requirements plus a safe margin and place an order with a bunker broker or bunker supplier. Instructions for refuelling are sent to the Master and to the Agent in the port concerned. The bunkering of ships is a billion dollar industry; the shipping sector burns some 250m tonnes of fuel per annum.

The largest tanker and bulk carrier will consume somewhere in the region of 60-70 tonnes of fuel per day. The largest container ship will burn about 400 tonnes of fuel per day. Bunker prices vary according to world crude oil prices. In 2012 fuel oil has fluctuated between $500 and $800 per tonne. It is generally a ship's largest expense and great efforts have been made in recent years to make main engines more efficient.

Chapter 7

Bunker testing

7.3 ADMIRALTY LAW

As in every industry it is inevitable that disputes will arise in the shipping sector. These of course vary in seriousness. Minor disputes can usually be settled by a shipbroker seeking and finding a compromise solution. The intervention of an august body such as the Baltic Exchange might be appropriate in more serious cases. Arbitration clauses are included in every charter party and this is both a cheap and a reasonably speedy resolution remedy.

When all else fails the parties resort to litigation. Admiralty law has cases going back centuries and is still used in London courts as yardsticks by which to measure the strength or weakness of the opposing sides. Cases are heard in front of Admiralty judges sitting at the Queen's Bench Division of the High Court in London. Admiralty legal practices are large and their caseloads heavy and the country's highest court, England's House of Lords has often been the final arbiter in complicated shipping cases.

Charter parties are governed by law and a clause in the charter might state that it is governed by English Law and proceedings will be heard in London. The USA and New York is another popular alternative.

The Royal Courts of Justice in London.

7.4 ARBITRATORS

As mentioned earlier, in charter parties an arbitration clause is normal. The concept of going to arbitration is that a dispute can be settled by shipping experts who will get around a table and debate the merits or otherwise of the case and come to a decision. It is intended that this type of dispute-resolution is both speedy and inexpensive. This is a typical clause; this one is to be found in the New York Produce Exchange (NYPE) form, a type of time-charter party.

'All disputes arising out of this contract shall be arbitrated at London and, unless the parties agree forthwith on a single Arbitrator, be referred to the final arbitrament of two Arbitrators carrying on business in London who shall be members of the Baltic Mercantile & Shipping Exchange and engaged in Shipping, one to be appointed by each of the parties, with power to such Arbitrators to appoint an Umpire. No award shall be questioned or invalidated on the ground that any of the Arbitrators is not qualified as above, unless objection to his action be taken before the award is made. Any dispute arising hereunder shall be governed by English Law.'

For disputes where the total amount claimed by either party does not exceed $100,000 the arbitration shall be conducted in accordance with the Small Claims Procedure of the London Maritime Arbitrators Association.

Other charter parties carry similar clauses. Different versions of arbitration apply to different maritime cases. Some categories of arbitration are binding, which means the parties agree to abide by the finding of the arbitrator. In other kinds of arbitration, called non-binding, the opinion arrived at is solely as a reference for further legal action.

Chapter 7

Arbitration should be quicker and cheaper than going to court.

7.5 CHART DEVELOPERS

An ancient mariner whom the author knew many years ago joined a ship in a hurry and proceeded on a trans-Atlantic voyage and found there were no Atlantic charts on board. He took an existing chart and on the back drew parallels of latitude and lines of longitude having calculated their spacing. He obtained the geographical position of relevant US ports and marked them on the chart. He consulted the Admiralty Ocean Passages and Admiralty Sailing Directions and was able to put enough information on his chart to be able to navigate to the pilot station nearest to their destination.

The Admiralty Hydrographic Department in South West England has been producing many more and much better charts than our ancient mariner and they are used throughout the world.

Ships running on a liner service will have folios of charts of relevance to their trade. A container ship exclusively trading in the trans-Pacific area will not usually have charts covering the rest of the world. In contrast, tramp ships will have folios covering most of the globe. Charts are supplied by agents in most major ports in the world and will be as correct and as up to date as possible.

What are called Notices to Mariners are issued weekly by various Hydrographic departments and contain chart corrections. The navigating officer on the ship, usually the Second Officer, is expected to keep the ship's charts up to date and Port State Control officers, under SOLAS provisions, are vigilant in spotting substandard work in this area.

Electronic charts are becoming more relied upon with ECDIS becoming compulsory on board ships in the next few years, initially with paper chart backup and then without. The benefit of electronic charts is that they can be corrected by the downloading of a large batch file and loading it into the navigation equipment to replace and update existing charts.

The shipping community has come a long way since Captain Cook charted most of the Pacific and Australia in the second half of the eighteenth century. Even now navigators praise his work. It is known that the charts he made of the St. Lawrence River and the coasts of New South Wales and Queensland are uncannily accurate.

Back office support

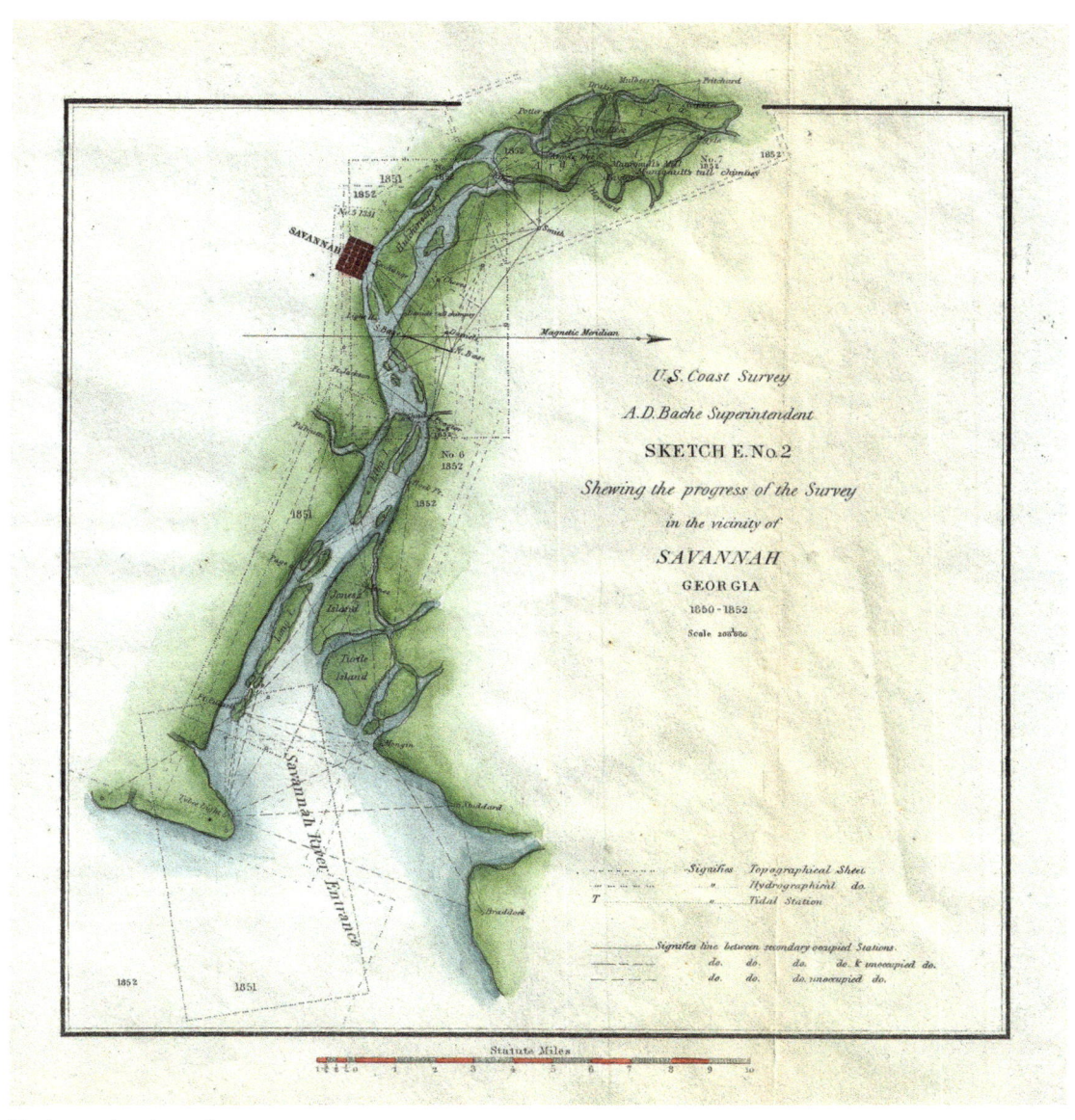

Early navigation chart.

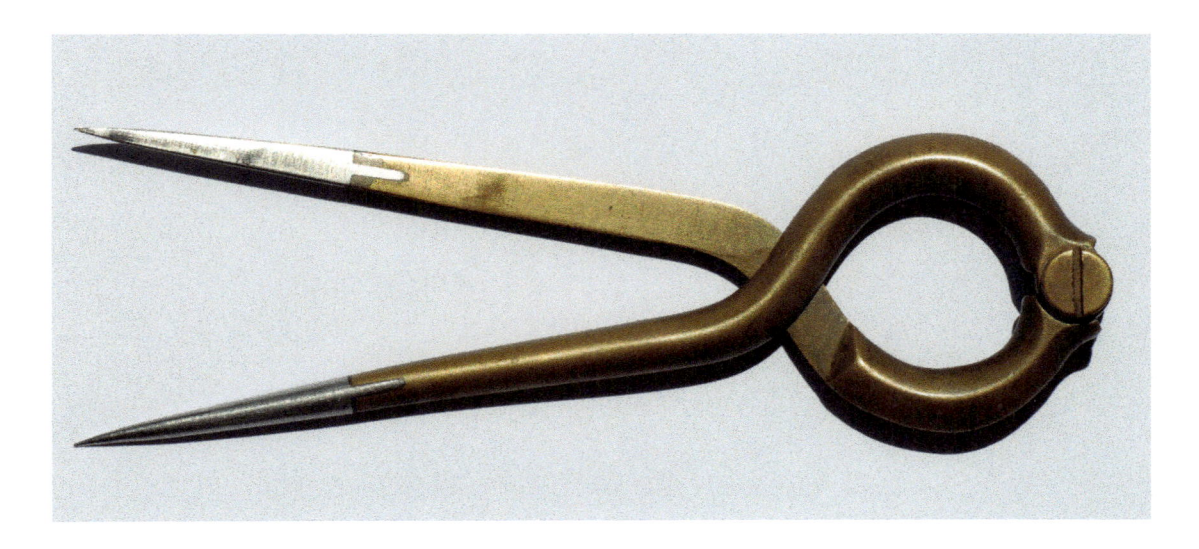

Chapter 7

Chapter 8
Law makers, regulators and enforcers

Security

Chapter 8

8.1 THE INTERNATIONAL MARITIME ORGANIZATION (IMO)

It has always been recognised that the best way of improving safety at sea is by developing international regulations that are followed by all shipping nations. From the mid-19th century onwards, a number of such treaties were adopted. Several countries proposed that a permanent international body should be established to promote maritime safety more effectively, but it was not until the establishment of the United Nations itself that these hopes were realised.

In 1948 an international conference in Geneva adopted a convention formally laying the foundations for the IMO. It started out as the Inter-Governmental Maritime Consultative Organization (IMCO), but the name was changed in 1982 to IMO. The IMO Convention entered into force in 1958 and the new organisation met for the first time the following year.

The purpose of the IMO is to provide machinery for cooperation among governments in the field of governmental regulation and practices relating to technical matters of all kinds affecting shipping engaged in international trade. It aims to encourage and facilitate the general adoption of the highest practicable standards in matters concerning maritime safety. It promotes the efficiency of navigation and the prevention and control of marine pollution from ships. The organisation is also empowered to deal with administrative and legal matters related to these purposes.

The IMO's first task was to adopt a new version of the International Convention for the Safety of Life at Sea (SOLAS). This considered to be the most important of all treaties dealing with maritime safety. This was achieved in 1960 and the IMO then turned its attention to such matters as the facilitation of international maritime traffic, load lines and the carriage of dangerous goods. The system of measuring the tonnage of ships was also revised.

But although safety was and remains the IMO's most important responsibility, a new problem began to emerge, that of pollution. The growth in the amount of oil being transported by sea and in the size of oil tankers was of particular concern and the Torrey Canyon disaster of 1967, in which 124,011 tonnes of oil was spilled, demonstrated the scale of the problem.

Torrey Canyon aground in the Isles of Scilly in 1967.

Law makers, regulators and enforcers

During the next few years the IMO introduced a series of measures designed to prevent tanker accidents and to minimize their consequences. It also tackled the environmental threat caused by routine operations such as the cleaning of oil cargo tanks and the disposal of engine room wastes, in tonnage terms a bigger menace than accidental pollution.

The most important of all these measures was the International Convention for the Prevention of Pollution from Ships, 1973, as modified by the Protocol of 1978 relating thereto. This title was abbreviated to MARPOL 73/78. It covers not only accidental and operational oil pollution but also pollution by chemicals, goods in packaged form, sewage, garbage and air pollution.

The IMO was also given the task of establishing a system for providing compensation to those who had suffered financially as a result of pollution. In 1969 and 1971, two treaties were adopted which enabled victims of oil pollution to obtain compensation much more simply and quickly than had been possible before. Both treaties were amended in 1992, and again in 2000, to increase the limits of compensation payable to victims of pollution. A number of other legal conventions have been developed since, most of which concern liability and compensation issues.

Also in the 1970s a global search and rescue system was initiated, with the establishment of the International Mobile Satellite Organization (IMSO). This has greatly improved the provision of radio and other messages to ships.

The Global Maritime Distress and Safety System (GMDSS) was adopted in 1988 and began to be phased in from 1992. In February 1999, the GMDSS became fully operational, so that now a ship that is in distress anywhere in the world can be virtually guaranteed assistance, even if the ship's crew do not have time to radio for help. Messages are transmitted automatically.

Chapter 8

Two initiatives in the 1990s are especially important insofar as they relate to the human element in shipping. On 1 July 1998 the International Safety Management Code (ISM) entered into force and became applicable to passenger ships, oil and chemical tankers, bulk carriers, gas carriers and cargo high speed craft of 500 gross tonnage and above. It became applicable to other cargo ships and mobile offshore drilling units of 500 gross tonnage and above from 1 July 2002.

On 1 February 1997, the 1995 amendments to the International Convention on Standards of Training, Certification and Watchkeeping for Seafarers (1978) entered into force. This was swiftly abbreviated to STCW. These amendments greatly improve seafarer standards and, for the first time, give the IMO itself powers to check government actions with parties required to submit information to the IMO regarding their compliance with the Convention. A major revision of the STCW Convention and Code was completed in 2010 with the adoption of the "Manila amendments to the STCW Convention and Code".

New conventions relating to the marine environment were adopted in the 2000s, including one on anti-fouling sytems (AFS 2001), another on ballast water management to prevent the invasion of alien species (BWM 2004) and another on ship recycling (Hong Kong International Convention for the Safe and Environmentally Sound Recycling of Ships, 2009).

The 2000s also saw a focus on maritime security, with the entry into force in July 2004 of a new, comprehensive security regime for international shipping, including the International Ship and Port Facility Security (ISPS) Code, made mandatory under amendments to SOLAS adopted in 2002.

In 2005, the IMO adopted amendments to the Convention for the Suppression of Unlawful Acts (SUA) Against the Safety of Maritime Navigation, 1988 and its related Protocol (the 2005 SUA Protocols).

As these IMO instruments have entered into force and been implemented, developments in technology and lessons learned from accidents have led to changes and amendments being adopted.

8.2 US CONGRESS

The Americans sometimes have what they call a knee-jerk reaction to events. This tendency emerged following the grounding of the VLCC Exxon Valdez in Alaska in 1989.

Exxon Valdez clean-up

Law makers, regulators and enforcers

The oil spill which resulted from this accident was comparatively minor compared with others that have occurred both before and since. It ranks only 37 in terms of the 36,426 tonnes of oil leaked. But pictures of sea mammals and fish being affected by nasty layers of crude oil had a life-changing affect on the American public as TV screens showed polluted snowy but previously pristine coastline.

Congress quickly passed the US Oil Pollution Act 1990. It was abbreviated to OPA-90 and contained a number of anti-pollution measures:

- Vessels trading to the USA had the produce certificates of financial responsibility;
- Be liable for $350m per oil spill plus clean-up costs;
- Mandating the development of response plans for individual tank vessels;
- Penalties for violations have a maximum of $250,000 and 15 years in prison;

The responsible party for a vessel from which oil is discharged, or which poses a substantial threat of a discharge, is liable for specified damages resulting from the discharged oil and removal costs incurred in a manner consistent with the National Contingency Plan (NCP).

Capitol Hill.

The US legislation has been followed by laws with similar aims and penalties in other areas of the world.

8.3 FLAG STATE

Flag State refers to the authority under which a country exercises regulatory control over the commercial vessels registered under its flag. This involves the inspection, certification, and issuance of safety and anti-pollution documentation.

The duties of a flag state have been covered quite widely by the IMO under various codes and conventions such as SOLAS, MARPOL, STCW, Collision Regulations, Loadline rules and the 1982 UN Convention on the Law of the Sea (UNCLOS).

Chapter 8

For example the latter stipulates under article 97 that: 'No arrest or detention of the ship, even as a measure of investigation, shall be ordered by any authorities other than those of the Flag State in relation to matters of collision or any other incident of navigation on the high seas.' And under article 217, the Flag State has overall responsibility for the implementation and enforcement of international maritime regulations for all ships granted the right to fly its flag.

8.5 PORT STATE OFFICIALS

These individuals oversee the adherence of all vessels entering its territorial waters and ports to international regulations. These include all international codes, conventions, rules, maritime regulations and undertakings. Some states have a separate organisation to fulfil these tasks. In the UK the Maritime and Coastguard Agency (MCA) performs these duties.

RVL Group aircraft chartered by the UK's Maritime and Coastguard Agency.

8.6 PORT STATE INSPECTORS

Every Port State Authority employs inspectors. These are often ex-Masters, experts who know their way around a ship. They have a programme of inspections which target vessels which have not been inspected for a period of time. A glance at international computer records will also tell them which vessels have been detained in the past. Some vessels flying flags from states which have had a previous bad record with substandard vessels are also targeted.

In some cases, the inspectors are tipped off by pilots who may have noticed out of date charts being used on the bridge. A Great Barrier Reef pilot in Australia boarded a ship and checked to see if things were in order. He looked into the prism which reflected readings from the main compass. He couldn't see anything. He went up to the monkey island and took the cover off the compass binnacle. There was no compass in there.

Back in the wheelhouse he asked the Master where the compass was. The Captain said that he hadn't noticed that the compass was missing, but he had only been in command of the ship for a short time. After the ship was detained by the Australian authorities, it emerged that this short time was in fact eight months.

Ship's binnacle.

Chapter 8

Chapter 9
Law of carriage

Scales of justice

Chapter 9

9.1 INTRODUCTION

In any area of business there are legal rules and there are legal remedies should any of the rules be transgressed or should any problems arise.

This is especially so in the shipping business where many transactions are only able to take place because of long-established legal customs and practices. It is vital, therefore, that students should be aware of the fundamental elements of the law of carriage of goods by sea which now includes those additional factors which the door-to-door aspects of containerisation have introduced.

Among the fundamentals, this chapter will discuss the important principles governing agreements as well as liabilities arising even where there is no actual agreement or contract.

Different countries have different legal systems and it is beyond the scope of this publication to examine closely those differences. A great deal of shipping law is, however, based upon English Law which will tend to dominate in this chapter.

Shipping is essentially an international business and the majority of the maritime nations of the world have agreed to conform to wide-ranging international Conventions by incorporating those conventions into their own legal systems.

9.2 FUNDAMENTALS OF ENGLISH LAW

English Law is a Common Law system which is to be contrasted with Civil Law systems which have all the law enacted as a set of codified legal principles. In a Common Law system, while there are, of course, many pieces of legislation enacted by the government, much of English Law is contained in a set of principles and rules taken from earlier decisions made by judges in court cases. You will often hear common law being referred to as Case Law.

Whenever one reads a report on a court case it is almost inevitable that there will be references to previous cases, perhaps even some going back to the nineteenth century. This is because no two cases are likely to be exactly similar and the judge, in reaching a decision, must consider the most comparable past cases in order to form a new decision.

9.2.1 The Civil Court Structure

In England there are three basic levels of courts.

1. The courts of 'First Instance' comprise (a) the County Courts, which deal in minor disputes, and (b) the High Courts for all other cases. The high courts have three divisions and the one dealing with commercial and maritime matters is called the Queen's Bench Division.

2. Above the courts of first instance is the Court of Appeal to which the losing party may go if it feels the first judge was wrong in reaching the decision. The Court of Appeal decisions are binding upon the courts of first instance.

3. The Supreme Court is the ultimate court of appeal and only very controversial cases are decided at that level. Its decisions are binding on all lower courts. It may overrule its own previous decisions although this rarely happens.

Also based in London is the Judicial Committee of the Privy Council which is the final court of appeal for the those United Kingdom dependent territories and those independent British Commonwealth countries which have retained this avenue of appeal upon achieving independence.

Those countries, including of course the United Kingdom, which are members of the European Union, have an even higher court of appeal which is the Court of Justice of the European Communities whose purpose is to rule on any cases which may be held to violate the Community treaties.

9.2.2 Criminal Law

All the foregoing refers to civil law; that is disputes between individuals or groups of individuals. Quite separate from civil law is criminal law which deals with acts harmful to the population. Criminal law is beyond the scope of this book except to remark that some wrongful acts within shipping business, for example fraud, are crimes and would be dealt with in the criminal courts. The criminal courts have their own tiered structure similar to, but quite separate from, the civil courts.

9.3 ARBITRATION

Arbitration is a private means of settling a dispute. The parties choose their own arbitrator, which may be a sole arbitrator, if they so agree, or each party chooses his own arbitrator. Under some systems if the two arbitrators cannot agree they appoint an umpire. In other places the appointment of a third arbitrator to form a tribunal of three is automatic. There are several centres of maritime arbitration but the most active are London and New York.

Originally arbitration was a very cheap and speedy way of settling disputes, with the arbitrators being themselves practising shipbrokers and their decisions being those of commercial men. But the world has become a more complicated and more litigious place, and arbitrations have involved professional lawyers arguing the case from both sides with the finer points of law appearing to be more important than a quick commercial settlement of an argument.

To overcome this problem and in an endeavour to regain arbitration's reputation for simplicity, both London and New York have introduced specific forms of arbitration which offer a quick and inexpensive alternative where the dispute is obviously suitable for a speedy solution.

Arbitration is not part of the country's public legal system although it is, of course, subject to governing legislation. With arbitration the parties are, in effect, choosing their own judges. Arbitration awards are final and binding upon the parties, the only appeal to the courts would be for a judicial review on a question of law.

9.4 THE CONTRACT

Fundamental to any business act is a contract and it is vital to be clear as to what constitutes a legally binding contract and how it comes about. There are three distinct components to a contract:

1. **The Offer.** An offer is a specific expression of willingness to enter into a contract on specified terms.
2. **Acceptance.** The offer must be accepted on the exact stated terms. This converts the offer into an agreement.
3. **Consideration.** For the agreement to become a contract there has to be a consideration. The person to whom the offer is made must give or promise to give something in return for the offer.
4. **Legality.** In order to be valid a contract must also be legally enforceable; contracts cannot relate to an activity which is not in itself lawful.

These four elements have to be technically present whether you are buying a bar of chocolate or chartering a 300,000 tonne tanker for twenty years. Furthermore, there need not be a physical object involved because a contract may be entered into to carry out a service such as a port agency.

Although there has to be a consideration for a contract to exist, there are no rules as to how much must be involved. A contract to sell a vintage Rolls Royce for £100 would be just as valid as one for £100,000, provided the parties willingly agreed. Indeed there does not even have to be actual money involved, there are still some leases for property in existence for which the annual rent is one penny, one cent or even something as small as a peppercorn.

The description of chartering negotiations are a perfect example of offer, acceptance with the consideration being the freight rate.

9.5 REMEDIES FOR BREACH OF CONTRACT

If one party or the other in a contract does not perform in accordance to that which was agreed, a breach has been committed and the injured party may seek redress.

If the breach of contract is a major failure, the injured party may simply withdraw from the contract and may seek damages. If the breach is a less important matter then the contract will continue to be valid but the injured party may seek damages.

Damages in this context mean the financial loss that has been suffered. In some cases, the amount of damages may be stipulated in the contract such as demurrage in a charter party in which case they are referred to as liquidated damages.

9.6 TORT

In the introduction it was mentioned that there may be liabilities even where no contract exists, and where no crime has been committed. Such a civil wrong is called a tort and it refers to an act or omission which causes another party damage in a situation where no contractual relationship exists. The party against whose person or property the tort was committed has the legal right to claim damages.

The type of tort which those in shipping business are most likely to encounter is negligence which is often described as a failure of a duty of care. A simple example would be where a ship allows an escape of oil which damages nearby property. The shipowner owed a duty of care to the nearby property owner, it was the oil spill that caused the damage and the property owner has the right to claim the cost of repairing that damage from the negligent shipowner.

Other torts include:

- Trespass, physical damage to another's property;
- Defamation, libel is a written or slander is a spoken statement which are held liable to damage a person's reputation;
- Conversion, allowing the possession of goods to pass into the hands of the wrongful owner. This could also be the crime of theft;
- Deceit, this would be fraud in a criminal case.

There are many instances in shipping business, for example, when an agent has control over what happens to goods even when they are not actually covered by a contract for which that agent is responsible, where a failure of a duty of care may occur and the agent may become liable for very heavy damages.

Another example could arise should a person be asked for information such as "You have done business with Mr So-and-So, is he all right financially?" If the answer given implies that Mr So-and-So is perfectly trustworthy financially without mentioning a suspicion that he is in fact a swindler, the enquirer could do business with Mr So-and-So and lose a lot of money. The enquirer could then have a legal case against the information provider who had a duty of care to give an honest and accurate reply.

Of course caution is needed here, the reply could have been "No, Mr So-and-So is a crook, have nothing to do with him" in which case the enquirer would not lose money but Mr So-and-So may get to hear what was said and sue the information giver for defamation of character, either slander or libel.

The right way to deal with such a situation is of course to say something like "I had no trouble when I dealt with Mr So-and-So but you should make formal enquiries elsewhere."

One of the worst situations, which falls under the heading of a tort of conversion, is when the agent releases discharged cargo to the wrong party. For instance, someone who did not present a valid bill of lading. In such a case the legitimate bill of lading holder can claim for the full value of the goods from the errant agent who will have no defence and no one else to turn to unless they are fully insured.

9.7 CONTRACTS RELATING TO THE CARRIAGE OF GOODS BY SEA

9.7.1 General

The way in which transport by sea is unique is that, whilst the ship is on passage, the goods loaded in it are:

(a) the ship's sole responsibility and

(b) inaccessible to anyone, of course except for the crew.

A great deal of the smooth operation of international trade depends upon taking proper advantage of these two facts.

There are two principal types of contracts for the carriage of goods by sea; the first being the charter party and the second the bill of lading.

9.7.2 Charter Parties

The charter party is a contract between the charterer and the shipowner with the rate and terms negotiated in an international market. Unless the parties choose specifically to incorporate any international conventions, such as the Hague-Visby Rules, a charter party is a stand-alone contract in which virtually all the intentions of the parties are set out.

We have already covered the different types of charter with some detail about the standard forms used. Such forms, with any amendments and additions upon which the parties may agree, set down in writing the full intentions of the parties, which are legally referred to as the express terms.

There are, however, certain terms in a charter party which are implied under common law and are referred to as implied terms.

In the case of a voyage charter some basic implied terms are:

On the part of the shipowner:

(a) that the ship is seaworthy.
(b) that the ship will proceed with reasonable despatch.
(c) that the ship will make no unjustifiable deviation.

On the part of the charterer:

(d) not to ship dangerous goods without the knowledge of the shipowner.

Chapter 9

In the case of a time charter:

(a) that the timecharterer will only use the vessel between good and safe ports.
(b) that dangerous goods will not be shipped without the knowledge of the shipowner.

There are no international conventions covering ships under charter. Although the parties may choose to incorporate some such clauses as:

1. stipulating that bills of lading covering the cargo carried, will be subject to the Hague Rules or the Hague-Visby Rules. The incorporating clause is often referred to as the Clause Paramount.

2. that General Average will be subject to the York Antwerp Rules which details how General Average should be applied and calculated.

General Average is a centuries-old convention which agrees that if the ship takes action which avoids a peril or reduces the effects of a peril, all parties must contribute to the cost of this action, known as the sacrifice according to the value of their participation in the venture. The incorporating clause is often referred to as the New Jason Clause.

Other standard clauses which are not strictly speaking derived from international convention but have wide acceptance may also be included such as a Both to Blame Collision Clause and a War Risk Clause.

9.8 LINER BILLS OF LADING

The second very common contract for carriage of good by sea is the bill of lading. Although the bill of lading is not an agreement but was evidence of a contract; the actual contract, very frequently only a verbal contract, having been made earlier. In the case of liner cargo, there is no equivalent of the charter party. While today there is often a degree of bargaining this tends almost always to be within the framework of the carrier's standard terms. Consequently it is rare for a written agreement to be produced for liner cargo and the vital document is the bill of lading.

Recall also the other functions of a bill of lading. It is a receipt for goods which covers both the quantity, which is set out in the body of the B/L and the quality which is covered by the words in apparent good order and condition. This enables the consignee to claim against the carrier if there is a shortage or if the cargo is damaged.

Today, most cargo is shipped in containers and in the case of full container loads (FCLs) the question of quantity and quality is in the hands of the shipper and this part of the B/L will simply contain a container number, together usually with the seal number, and the words said to contain when describing the cargo. The consignee then has no claim against the carrier provided the container is undamaged and the seal is intact unless it can be proved that the contents had been damaged due to container having been badly handled.

With less than container loads (LCL cargo) the carrier's responsibility as regards quantity and quality is the same as for break-bulk or conventional cargo.

Note also in the case of break-bulk cargo, that technically, the B/L does not begin to operate until the cargo crosses the ship's rail at the time of loading. With container cargo, however, the receipt element of the B/L and also the carrier's liability, comes into effect much sooner, possibly at the shipper's premises. For this reason, it will be recalled, a container B/L states 'Received' rather than 'Shipped' above the carrier's signature and the B/L needs a further endorsement to say when shipment actually took place in order to become a 'shipped on board B/L'.

Finally the B/L is a document of title; the definition of title in this context is 'the right to ownership of property with or without actual possession'.

Refer back to the preamble to this section of the chapter where it was pointed out that no one has access to the cargo whilst it is afloat. Therefore, during this time the B/L is able to be a negotiable document, enabling a named consignee to sell the cargo and to pass title to the cargo by endorsing the B/L by signing it on the back. There is no limit to the number of times a B/L, and also title to the cargo, can change hands in this manner so long as it takes place while the cargo is still on the ship.

Payment for the cargo may have been arranged via the banking system through the medium of a documentary letter of credit in which case the second part of the B/L's role as a document of title comes into play, this time as security for payment. In such a case, the B/L is not made out to a named consignee but in that part of the B/L the words 'To Order' appear. Such a document has to be endorsed by the actual shipper and thereafter does not need any further endorsement because it is now 'open' and title to the goods belongs to anyone holding the B/L – theoretically they can claim the goods even if they found the B/L in the street. In the real world, shipping lines and their agents are very wary of handing goods to anyone who has obtained the B/L illegally. Most countries recognise the crime of stealing by finding.

Although title to the goods may be transferred from one to another, the actual contract remains between the original shipper and the carrier. A way had to be found to ensure that the rights and liabilities under the contract also pass to the new consignee or endorsee. To this end the UK originally passed the *Bill of Lading Act 1855*. The evolution in liner shipping meant that this needed up-dating and it was replaced with the *Carriage of Goods by Sea Act 1992*.

Many find this title a misnomer because there is already a *Carriage of Goods by Sea Act 1971* which is the act with which the UK ratified the Hague/Visby rules. So it is vital to remember that the *1992 Act replaces the B/L Act of 1855 and does not affect the 1971 Act*.

The *Carriage of Goods by Sea Act 1992* (as did the 1855 B/L Act) empowers the consignee to sue the carrier and also subject the consignee to the liabilities in respect of the goods as if the contract had been made between the consignee and the carrier. The 1992 Act corrects various anomalies in the 1855 Act that the passage of time has revealed as well as taking Sea Waybills and Delivery orders into consideration.

9.9 THE HAGUE/VISBY RULES

Whereas there is some degree of equality of bargaining strength between an owner and a charterer which only varies according to the fluctuation of the market, liner shippers seldom have such power.

In the distant past, owners of ships carrying general cargo were able to exert their bargaining strength over shippers by imposing contract terms which allowed the shipowners to exempt themselves from all manner of negligence. Shippers rebelled and lobbied governments to introduce legislation in order to curb this abuse of shipowner power. This resulted in a hotch-potch of laws across the world which, in such an essentially international business as shipping, created chaos.

Governments, therefore, came together to discuss the drafting of an international convention. It was not until 1921 that agreement was reached and the Hague Rules came into being. These were ratified by almost all the world's maritime nations; in the UK it was ratified by the *Carriage of Goods by Sea Act 1924*.

Then, largely due to the introduction of containerisation and changing values, the Maritime Law Committee of the International Law Association agreed to amend the Hague Rules with the Brussels Protocol of 1958 and the amended Hague Rules became known as the Hague/Visby Rules (refer again to Appendix 29). These rules again found favour with most maritime nations and the UK ratified the rules with the *Carriage of Goods by Sea Act 1971* which replaced (repealed) the 1924 Act.

The Hague/Visby Rules only apply to goods carried under a Bill of Lading or similar document. They do not apply to a charter party unless specifically incorporated.

Chapter 9

In the Rules the term 'carrier' is used throughout so that it includes owner or charterer who enters into a contract of carriage with a shipper. In the simplest terms, the Rules set out:

(a) the duties of the carrier to provide a seaworthy and cargoworthy ship at the beginning of the voyage. This is not an absolute liability, if the ship becomes unseaworthy during the course of the voyage want of due diligence has to be proved;

(b) the carrier must provide a bill of lading or similar document;

(c) there must be no unjustifiable or unreasonable deviation;

(d) the shipper guarantees the accuracy of the cargo details supplied by him;

(e) there is a list of things for which the carrier shall not be liable, these are matters which are clearly not under the carrier's control;

(f) there is a limit to the amount of compensation the carrier has to pay in the event of loss or damage. This is the equivalent of saying 'This is where my insurance stops so this is where yours should start'. The maximum amount is per package and in the Hague/Visby Rules the definition of package when containerisation is involved has been covered;

(g) there is a Himalaya clause incorporated in the rules;

(h) a claim for loss or damage shall be time-barred unless suit is brought within one year of delivery or the date when they should have been delivered.

Bear in mind that, now the vast majority of manufactured goods are being carried in containers, a Combined Transport B/L covers far more than simply carriage by sea. It now includes all the other ancillary transportation elements which comprise what is now termed intermodalism.

There are international conventions covering the carriage by road, referred to as The CMR Convention. The initials stand for *Convention relative au contrat de transport des Marchandises par vois de Route*.

Similarly carriage by rail within Europe is covered by The CIM Convention *(Convention International concernant le transport de Marchandises par chemin de fer)*.

The details of these conventions are beyond the scope of this publication. It is important to know that the rules and limitations of liability of these modes of transport come into effect if loss or damage occurs on road, respectively on rail, but that if the precise place where the problem arose is unknown, the Hague Visby Rules shall apply.

9.10 HIMALAYA CLAUSE

Reference was made earlier that the Hague-Visby Rules include a Himalaya Clause. This clause brings agents and other servants of the owner under the limits of liability protection of the Bill of Lading. The clause is named after a passenger ship which created a legal landmark in the shipping world in 1954. A lady passenger, a Mrs Adler was injured when descending a gangway from the ship; the gangway had been inadequately secured. She found that, under the contract evidenced by her passenger ticket, she could not claim damages from the shipowner but she successfully sued the ship's Master (a Captain Dickson) in *tort*, as he had failed in his duty of care. Not only was this a classic example of the law of *tort* in action, but it was also a demonstration of vicarious liability; the definition of vicarious is acting or done for another. Securing the gangway was not part of the captain's own duties, but it was the job of someone under his command.

This case (*Adler v Dickson 1954*) sent a shockwave through the whole shipping business world. As it was realised that the same device could be used to circumvent the limits of liability, which the Hague Rules conferred upon the bill of lading. Therefore, it was that bills of lading were hastily re-drafted to include a clause which extended the protection of the B/L to all those directly working for the owner.

The reasonableness of such a clause was generally accepted throughout the shipping world so that, when the time came to up-date the Hague Rules by producing the Hague-Visby Rules, the situation was fully covered by the inclusion of the four clauses which comprise Article IV*bis* in the Rules. Note that Clause 4 in that article does not protect the servant or agent if it is proved that the damage resulted from an act, done with the intent to cause damage or recklessly.

9.11 THE HAMBURG RULES

The United Nations Commission for Trade and Development (UNCTAD), whose brief is principally to look after the affairs of less developed nations, held a meeting in Hamburg to consider the carriage of goods by sea in 1978. The meeting produced a rival to the Hague/Visby Rules entitled the Hamburg Rules.

The object of these rules was to favour non-maritime nations which tend to be cargo-owning countries. This is apparent when you see the limited number of nations which have ratified the Hamburg Rules.

Some of the principal differences include:

(a) Hague/Visby only operates as goods pass the ships rail in and out but Hamburg covers the whole period during which the carrier is in charge of the goods. So, for example, applies before and after loading/discharge;

(b) the carriage of live animals and deck cargo are completely excluded from the provisions of Hague/Visby but there is a qualified inclusion in Hamburg;

(c) there is no provision for loss due to delay in Hague/Visby but with Hamburg the carrier is liable for losses due to delay unless he can prove the delay was entirely beyond his control;

(d) the amount of compensation for loss or damage is much higher in Hamburg under limitation of liability provision;

(e) the time bar is two years under Hamburg against one year in Hague/Visby;

(f) Hague Rules apply to goods loaded in a signatory state. Hamburg rules apply when goods are loaded or discharged in a signatory state. This may lead to conflicts under the B/L where the loading port is Hague-Visby and the discharging port is under Hamburg Rules.

9.12 THE ROTTERDAM RULES

The matter of international law relating to the carriage of goods by sea has never been straightforward and it is still somewhat confused today. In addition to the Hague, Hague/Visby and Hamburg rules there are a whole variety of domestic legislation around the world, that picks parts from each or adds in elements from outside. In 2009 the UN completed work on a revised new text that will supersede the Hamburg rules. It will address the argument that whereas the Hague rules were biased in favour of the shipowners, the Hamburg rules allowed the pendulum to swing too far the other way.

These new rules are referred to as 'The Rotterdam Rules' but the text needs to be ratified by nations and adopted into national law before they will become effective. The Rotterdam Rules are the first to address the issue of multi-modal transport. While they have received an enthusiastic reception from many organisations around the world representing both shipowners and cargo interests, at least one body, The European Shippers' Council, has expressed concerns and in June 2009 were requesting that the rules should be reconsidered.

It is unlikely that the Rotterdam Rules will become the accepted standard for some time because of the protracted process of ratification and incorporating into statute. However, their existence should not be overlooked because it is conceivable that some parties may choose to adopt them as a freely negotiated contractual obligation. The final text of the Rotterdam Rules was agreed in 2009 and, in September that year, the rules were open for signatories. Currently the treaty has been signed by 24 countries, including the USA, Norway and the Netherlands and a number of more minor nations. As soon as the treaty is ratified by 20 nations it will take effect. To date only one country, namely Spain, has ratified the Rotterdam Rules. The general feeling is that it will be at least 2015 before the Rules are fully ratified, even by the present signatories.

9.13 AGENCY

All the six disciplines in the commercial shipping world are forms of agency, that is to say carrying out work on behalf of a principal except, of course, where the work is done by a department in the principal's own office. An agent's function is to bring their principal into contractual relationships with third parties.

9.13.1 Creation of a Relationship of Agency

An agency can be created:

(a) by express agreement.

(b) by implication/conduct

(c) by necessity, that is where a person is entrusted with another person's property and a definite and commercial necessity arises to deal with that property and it is impossible to obtain the property-owners's instructions.

9.13.2 Rights and Duties imposed as between Agent and Principal

Duties of an Agent:

(a) to exercise due diligence in performance of his duties.

(b) to apply any special skill which he professes to have.

(c) to render account.

(d) not to make a secret profit doing so is a crime in many countries. An example could be where the agent agrees that the stevedore should inflate their account to the shipowner and pay the excess as a secret commission to the agent.

Duties of a Principal:

(a) to remunerate the agent.

(b) to indemnify the agent for liabilities incurred in the execution of their authority. This not only includes reimbursing for expenses incurred on the principal's behalf but also protecting the agent against mis-directed arrows, which includes legal action directed against the agent when it should have been directed against the principal.

9.14 BREACH OF WARRANTY OF AUTHORITY

When an agency deals on behalf of their principal the agency is warranting to the third party that they have its principal's authority to do so. If they deal without that authority be it actual, implicit or of necessity, then they are in breach of the warranty of authority.

The agent can be in breach deliberately, that is they knew they were doing so, or was reckless as to whether or not they were in breach. They can also be in breach through negligence. For example, misreading the terms upon which they were authorised to offer a ship for a cargo and the subsequent fixture is not on the terms the owner intended.

In either of these cases the agent, by warranting they had authority to do what they did, will be liable to the third party for any loss so caused; mistakes have to be paid for.

There is another way that breach of warranty of authority operates which is less easy to understand. Imagine that you are a broker negotiating with a charterer on behalf of an owner based in another country. Now suppose that the authority to make an offer to the charterer comes not directly from the owner but from a broker in the owner's country and it is that broker who misreads the authority and passes to you a firm offer with a mistake in it. In good faith you make this offer to the charterer *warranting you have to owner's authority to do so*. If a fixture is concluded with this error in it and the charterer sustains a loss they will seek recompense and the law says you have to pay.

This may seem unfair because you have made no mistake but the view the law takes is that it would be quite wrong for the charterer to suffer. It would be equally wrong for the charterer to have to proceed against the foreign broker who made the mistake as the charterer had no direct contact with that broker. No, the faulty offer came from you so you have to pay the charterer's damages, this is breach of warranty of authority without negligence. All you can do is proceed against the overseas broker who made the error to recover what you have had to pay out. Fortunately agents and brokers can insure, usually through their P & I Club, against breach of warranty of authority, with or without negligence and in view of the way one cannot otherwise protect oneself against a without negligence situation, such insurance is a wise precaution.

9.15　PROTECTION AND INDEMNITY ASSOCIATIONS

P & I Clubs as they are called are principally concerned with providing shipowners with insurance against third party risks. They originated in the 19th century because commercial insurers and underwriters were not prepared to offer the full cover for these risks because of their open ended nature. P & I cover is arranged on a basis of "mutuality" which is to say that the clubs are non-profit making entities whose funds are contributed by the members and are named calls. Members present their claims for sums which they have settled with the third party and what they have paid is reimbursed to them; this is the indemnity element of the clubs. Should the claims on the club exceed the funds available, the club will make a supplementary call to obtain the necessary extra money from the members.

The protection element involves providing legal advice to members and fighting claims which are considered to be wrong or excessive.

The main P & I Clubs are those of shipowners. The third party claims involved, include such things as:

- personal injury claims by people working on the ships;
- damage to property such as colliding with a jetty;
- cargo claims from consignees who are claiming short delivery or damage to their cargo (probably the most active section of claims).

There are also P & I Clubs for charterers and for shipbrokers. The latter are principally concerned with professional indemnity insurance, that is insuring people in shipping business against claims made against them for negligence.

Recently there has been a tendency among some owners to return to commercial insurance cover for their third party risks.

Chapter 9

Chapter 10

Where the money comes from

Capesize bulk carrier

Chapter 10

10.1 INTRODUCTION

10.1.1 The six sectors

By far the largest sector of the shipping market is the dry-cargo sector. It divides into several subdivisions. The basic and most common is the dry bulk market. As the name suggests, the vessels involved carry cargoes in bulk. This means there are no boxes involved; no bags, no containers, nothing wrapped or enclosed, just the cargo loaded straight into the ship's hold.

The largest quantity of cargoes carried on ships comprise coal, iron ore, grain, bauxite, phosphate, alumina and other mineral ores. The amount carried in the course of a year is more than 1.7 Bn tonnes. Bulk carriers are also used for the carriage of sawn timber as well as logs, woodchips and paper pulp. Metal scrap and new steel coils, bars and rolled steel slabs are all carried in bulk.

During 2011, the closest whole year figures available, bulk carriers attracted the following daily earnings:

	Capesize	Panamax	Handymax	Handysize
Average voyage earnings	15,679	13,895	13,814	10,884
Numbers of vessels trading	1,352	2,206	2,463	3,049
Total daily fleet earnings	21.198m	30.650m	34.024m	33.185m
Annual fleet earnings	7,737m	11,187m	12,419m	12,113m

Figures: Clarkson Research Services.

It can therefore be seen that bulk carriers working in the market earned about $43.456 Bn. This is equal to the gross GDP of countries like Serbia or Lithuania.

Capesize bulk carrier at Suez Canal Bridge

Where the money comes from

10.1.2 Containerships

Most seaborne manufactured goods are carried in freight containers. These are mostly boxes of forty feet (12.2m) long. Some cargoes are carried in 20 foot containers while others are carried in specialised containers. These include refrigerated containers, tank boxes, flat bed or over-height containers. The shipper charges a freight rate per container. The numbers of containers shipped are expressed in TEUs.

In 2011, more than 151m containers were shipped by sea. This is up from nearly 140m teu in 2010.

	Panamax	Sub-Panamax	Handysize	Small Handy	Feedermax
Average voyage earnings	13,250	9,942	6,800	6,133	4,535
Numbers of vessels trading	930	959	710	1,279	1,210
Total daily fleet earnings	12.322m	9.534m	4.828m	7.844m	5.487m
Annual fleet earnings	4,497.5m	3,479.9m	1,762.2m	2,863m	2,003m

Figures: Clarkson Research Services.

It can therefore be seen that container ships working in the market earned about $14.6 Bn. This ignores and excludes earnings from post-Panamax vessels which carry in excess of 8,000-teu each with the largest currently trading, lifting 14,700-teu. These figures are not available.

Panamax bulk carrier 'Pasha Bulker' aground off Newcastle NSW.

10.1.3 Crude tankers

The carriage of crude is not restricted to VLCCs, although this is where the majority of cargoes are traded. VLCCs tend to load in the Middle East to both eastern and western destinations. They also load in West Africa, the Mediterranean and the North Sea. They load about two million barrels of oil. They also carry backhaul cargoes from Europe and the Caribbeans to the Far East.

Chapter 10

Suezmax tankers carry about one million barrels of oil. They load in West Africa, the Mediterranean, the Black Sea and Northern Europe for discharge generally within the Western Hemisphere. East of Suez they load in the Middle East for discharge to India and East Asia.

Aframax tankers load in the Caribbeans, the North Sea, the Baltic, the Black and Mediterranean Seas, the Middle East and Indonesia. They discharge in most areas of the world.

During 2011, the most recent whole year figures available, bulk carriers attracted the following daily earnings:

	VLCC	Suezmax	Aframax	Panamax
Average voyage earnings	16,858	19,217	13,528	10,535
Numbers of vessels trading	578	445	913	412
Total daily fleet earnings	9.744m	8.551m	12.351m	3.340m
Annual fleet earnings	3,557m	3,121m	4,508m	1,219m

Figures: Clarkson Research Services.

It can therefore be seen that crude oil tankers working in the market earned about $12.405 Bn.

Tanker alongside and discharging.

10.1.4 Clean tankers

These vessels vary in size between a carrying capacity of 15,000 tonnes to 75,000 tonnes. Thus they trade from refinery ports where products are produced, to the ports where the consumers or the manufacturing centres are based. Thus there are almost no coastal or riverside centres of population where these ships do not pay visits.

	LR1	LR2	MR	Handy
Average voyage earnings	10,462	7,753	7,587	12,644
Numbers of vessels trading	2,100		3,323	
Total daily fleet earnings	19.126m		33.614m	
Annual fleet earnings	6,981m		12,269m	

Figures: Clarkson Research Services.

It can therefore be seen that clean product tankers earned about $19,250 Bn. But these figures are rather speculative since it is difficult to determine which ships are trading in clean or dirty products or indeed, chemicals or vegetable oils, the figures are no more than an estimate.

Oil tankers in port

10.1.5 Gas ships

Gas ships are divided into two classes, those that carry petrochemical gases produced by oil refinery processes and the rest which carry natural gases such as ethane and methane. There are no available earnings figures for Liquefied Natural Gas (LNG) ships but given their high construction costs, they should attract a daily rate of about $60,000. Thus the fleet of 373 ships could have earned as much as $8 Bn in 2011.

LPG ships are slightly easier to calculate in their size categories in cubic metres:

Chapter 10

	60,000+	40-60,000	20-40,000	5-20,000	Up to 5,000
Average daily earnings	25,869	22,512	20,640	17,949	9,487
Numbers of ships	142	19	115	283	658
Daily fleet earnings	3.673m	0.428m	2.374m	5.080m	6.242m
Annual earnings	1,341m	156m	867m	1,854m	4,107m

Figures: Clarkson Research Services

LPG carriers took home about $8.3 Bn. Therefore added to the estimate of $8 Bn earned by LNG carriers, the gas sector earned about $16.3 Bn.

LNG carrier

10.1.6 Offshore Industry

There are no figures available relating to earnings of offshore support vessels, drilling rigs and offshore oil production platforms. All we can surmise is that in 2011 anchor handling tug and supply vessels earned an average $43,000 per day and there were 2,917 of them at the end of the year. Platform support vessels averaged $15,700 daily and there were 2,290 trading in December 2011. We are not certain that all these ships were employed for 365 days per year. So if we estimate that they were employed for 300 days in 2011 we have the following figures:

	Anchor Handling Tug/Supply	Sue Platform Support Vessel
Average voyage earnings	$43,000	$15,700
Numbers of vessels trading	2,917	2,290
Total daily fleet earnings	125.431m	35.953m
Annual fleet earnings	37,629m	10,786m

Figures: Clarkson Research Services

Where the money comes from

Modern offshore support vessel.

Drilling for oil offshore.

It can be seen that if the support vessels earn about $50 Bn per year, the hundreds of drilling rigs and production platforms must also make a huge financial contribution to the shipping sector. Some rigs and platforms attract a daily hire rate of as much as half a million dollars per day.

Chapter 10

10.1.7 Unsung heroes

The vessels we have not covered are the passenger ships such as ferries and cruise liners. Pure car carriers and truck carriers as well as Ro-Ro ships and heavy lift vessels. It is impossible to even guess what earnings these sectors bring in.

Earnings in the other sectors amount to more than $155 Bn per annum. This is equal to the GDP of a country the size of Hungary or the Ukraine. It could possibly be as big as a country the size of Pakistan or Portugal.

10.2 TYPES OF EMPLOYMENT

One of the popular types of employment among tankers and dry cargo ships is a timecharter. The vessel is taken on by a charterer for a period of time. The owner pays for all the operating costs apart from the bunkers and port charges and any dues or taxes levied on the cargo. The charterer operates the ship in its own programme rather than the owner's. Hire is usually paid monthly or semi-monthly in advance.

Another type of charter is a voyage charter. The owner charters the ship to a charterer for a voyage. During negotiations, agreed terms include the loading port range and discharging port range. For example it could be loading Northwest Europe Gibraltar-Hamburg range. It could be discharging US Atlantic Coast and/or US Gulf. Also negotiated is the date or range of dates the vessel is to present for loading and the freight rate, usually stated in US dollars per tonne. The cargo is loaded and discharged free of cost to the ship-owner. The owner is obliged to transport the cargo at the best speed weather and safe navigation permitting. Freight is usually paid either a certain number of days after loading, before breaking bulk or on completion of discharge. The owner pays for the voyage costs.

In dry cargo some vessels such as multi-purpose ships are fixed on what are called liner terms. In this case the vessel is chartered for a cargo but the agreed freight is inclusive of carriage and the cost of cargo handling at the loading and discharging ports. The ship can carry a large number of different cargoes, all negotiated on their own freight rates.

Another type of charter is called a bareboat charter. Is this style of employment, the charterer takes over the ship and crews it, fuels it, operates it, maintains it, insures it, dry-docks it, keeps its certificates up to date and to all intents and purposes uses the ships as if the charterer was actually the owner. In return the actual owner receives an agreed monthly hire amount. At the end of the charter period, the vessel is given back or redelivered in the same condition as it was in at the beginning of the charter, fair wear and tear accepted.

There is also a demise charter. This is a bareboat charter where the vessel is delivered to the charterer at the beginning of the vessel's life and redelivered when its useful life has ended.

Where the money comes from

Post-panamax 9,500-teu container ship, 'MSC Sindy'

10.2.1 Basis of payment

To put it in its basic terms the shipowner is paid by the cargo factor. Here are the different ways in which this done.

Timecharter	All normal types of ship	Monthly in advance Semi-monthly in advance Monthly in arrears
	Dry cargo ships	With the option of a ballast bonus
Voyage charter	Tankers	Worldscale terms Lumpsum US$ per tonne
Voyage charter	Dry cargo	US$ per tonne
Liner terms	Multi-purpose and liner types	US$ per unit of cargo
Bareboat and demise charter	Any type	US$ Monthly in advance
Timecharter	Offshore support vessels	GB pounds (£) per day

Offshore support ships are paid in Pounds sterling

10.3 COMMISSION PAYMENTS

Shipbrokers earn a commission for the work they do. In the tanker industry it is usually 1¼% paid by the owner on freight, deadfreight and demurrage in the case of voyage charters. In the case of timecharters and bareboat charters, it is paid as a percentage of the charter hire.

It is a similar picture in the dry cargo sector and the container trade. But what occurs in the tanker sector, but is even more prevalent in the dry cargo sector is what is called an address commission. In effect this is a discount on the agreed freight or charter hire. It can be as large as 5% and is a significant reduction in the owner's earnings.

Most ship-owners are very good at paying commissions. But there is the odd exception. In a very good market when hires and freight rates are high, some owners claim that the actual amount of the commission is too much. In effect the owners feel they are giving the broker too much income.

Then of course, when the market is poor, an owner might claim that the freight is below their ship's break-even level and they might claim that they cannot afford such a large amount. So in some instances, the broker cannot win.

Chapter 11
Accounts

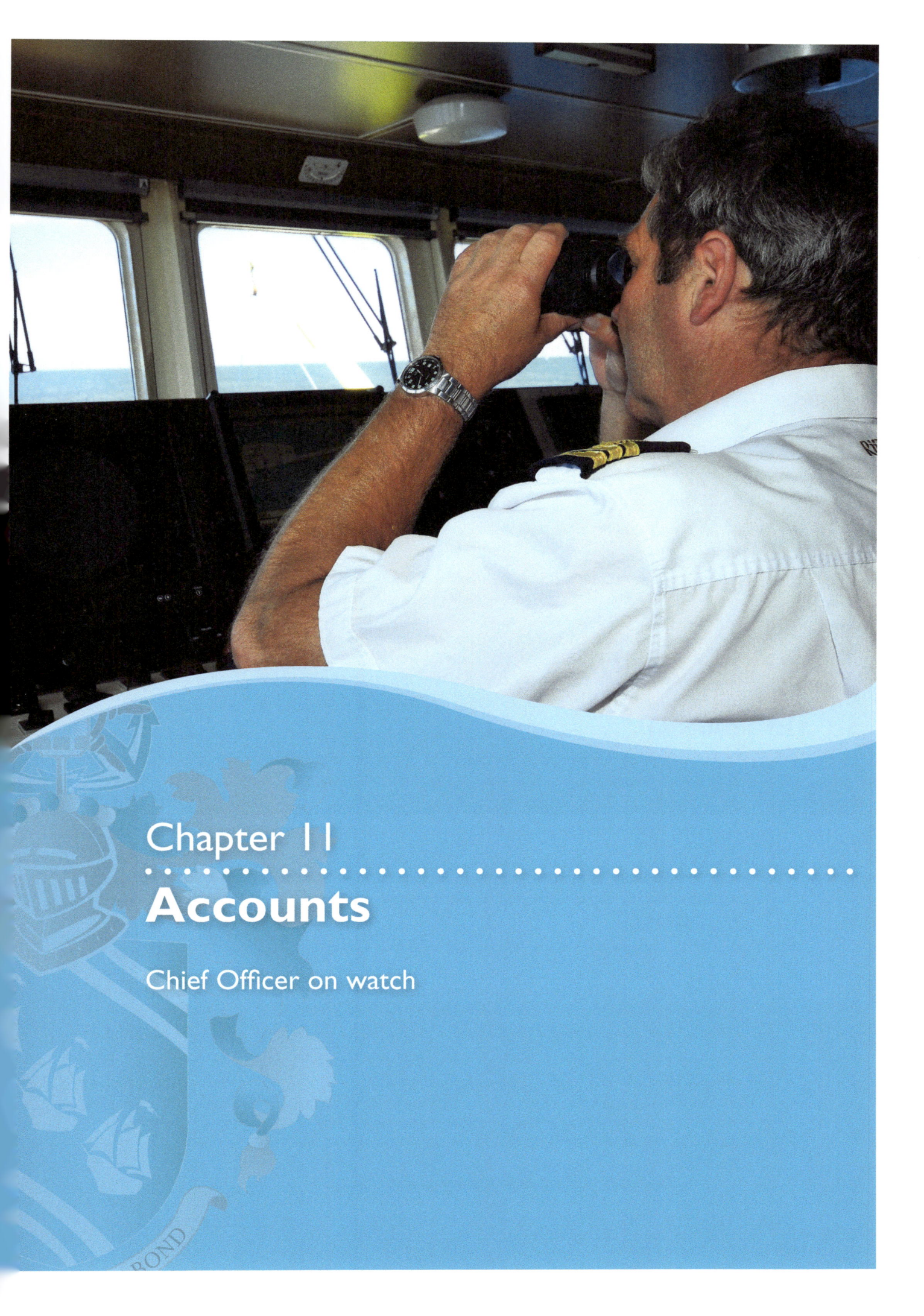

Chief Officer on watch

Chapter 11

11.1 INTRODUCTION

The famous Greek shipowner, Aristotle Onassis, is once alleged to have said that successful shipowning was 95% careful accounting. This view is perhaps reinforced when one considers how many prosperous Far East shipowners are, by background, financiers or bankers.

It is self-evident that if an enterprise spends more than it earns, it will not survive; unless, of course, it is subsidised from public funds such as a country bus service or an island ferry service which is run as a social service.

Whether intended as a profitable business or as a non-profit making undertaking it is necessary to produce records of income and expenditure more usually known as a set of books. This chapter does not attempt to be a training course in accounting or bookkeeping but seeks to provide an introduction into the basics of accounting matters in a shipping business context.

11.2 ACCOUNTING

Accounting is the complete package of all the planning and managing of the company's financial affairs. Bookkeeping is a part of accounting, its particular objects being:

1. To have a permanent record of all mercantile transactions;

2. To show the effect of each transaction and the combined effect of all the transactions upon the financial position of the enterprise.

The rest of the accounting process involves many other things including, for example, deciding what commercial activities are viable, that is practicable from an economic point of view, deciding what capital items to purchase, raising money to purchase capital items, ensuring there is always sufficient money or cash available to pay accounts at the correct time, investing surplus money so that it earns interest when not needed for immediate use. In fact anything which affects the financial position of the company comes under the heading of accounts.

11.3 CAPITAL

Capital in bookkeeping terms is the total value of all the company's fixed assets, investments, and cash, these are called assets. Assets are divided into fixed assets and current assets.

Capital is the money required to start a commercial enterprise and more may be required from time to time to maintain its momentum or to increase the range of its activities.

Capital is needed for two basic purposes, first to purchase any items of machinery or equipment i.e. anything which will become a fixed asset such as, for example, a ship. Capital is also required to run the company, to pay wages and salaries, to settle bills for rent etc this sort of capital is called working capital.

Capital, for whatever purpose, has to be raised. This can be by means of letting other people become owners of part of the company which will be dealt with later in this chapter when the structure of companies is discussed. Or, capital can be raised by borrowing the money from a bank or other financial institution, this is often referred to as loan capital and the borrower has to pay the lender interest at an agreed percentage per annum as well as repay the loan in agreed instalments.

Interest is the percentage of the capital sum that the borrower pays the lender for the use of the money borrowed. Although borrowing among individuals may be frowned upon, borrowing and lending is an essential element of commercial life. A company may find it has, temporarily, more cash than it needs for its immediate purposes and will deposit this with a bank so that it earns interest rather than lying idle. On another occasion it may have a temporary shortage of ready cash which will require a short-term loan from the bank known as an overdraft; a well-run company can usually negotiate a substantial overdraft facility.

There is a special type of borrowing which is often used for buying such things as houses and ships. This is by means of a mortgage which is the name of the deed or agreement signed by the owner of the ship which, in exchange for the loan of a substantial amount of its cost, pledges the ship as security for the loan. This means that if the owner, known as the borrower, cannot meet the loan repayments and interest charges the lender may foreclose on the mortgage which means the lender can take possession of the ship. It is important to note that it is the borrower who gives the mortgage to the lender so that the borrower, the shipowner in this case, becomes the mortgagor and the bank or finance house who takes the mortgage becomes the mortgagee.

A ship, or a building or a piece of machinery is capital and is classified as a fixed asset. Many companies invest in associated businesses, for example a shipping company might invest in part of a terminal operating company. Such an investment, indeed any long-term investment, will also be classified as a fixed asset.

11.4 CREDIT

Goods and services in the commercial world are most frequently provided without immediate payment; the recipient of the goods is given credit. A most important function of bookkeeping is keeping track of this credit. When goods and/or services are supplied, an account is rendered; this may be called an invoice. This document gives details of the goods or services provided and the cost; there may be a reference on the invoice as to when payment should be made or the length of time permitted between supply and payment may be by mutual agreement between the two parties.

Those who have supplied goods or services and who are awaiting settlement of their invoices are creditors. When the accounts are paid, the outgoing money is referred to as expenditure.

Those who owe money against outstanding invoices are debtors, when they have settled their accounts the money received is referred to as income or revenue.

The function of bookkeeping is to record all outgoing and incoming accounts which are entered in ledgers. In years gone by these would have been large heavy books into which transactions were recorded in ink. Most major enterprises now keep all accounts by computer but the word 'ledger' is still often used to refer to those parts of the system that record the issuing and/or receiving of invoices. The bookkeeping process then records when the invoices are settled and the traditional name for that record quite logically was the cash book, in computerised systems sometimes also referred to as transaction lists.

From time to time the totals of money received and money paid out and the totals of money owed by debtors and money owed to creditors are calculated and the result is either a profit or a loss. In most countries, such an account is simply called the Profit and Loss Account and such an account, covering the sum of all the transactions during the past year, has to be produced annually by limited companies, it has to be checked by an independent accountant called an auditor and then submitted to the government; it may eventually become available for public scrutiny.

At the same time as the Profit and Loss Account is published another account called the Balance Sheet also has to be produced. The Balance Sheet sets out the value of all the company's assets and liabilities at the end of that particular trading year. Assets as referred to earlier are the value of goods, investments, money due to be received from debtors and cash the company has at that moment in time. Liabilities include moneys due to be paid to creditors, loans which still have to be repaid and amounts due to the shareholders who subscribed the money with which the company was formed.

In the Balance Sheet assets are valued at the amount of money used to purchase them. Most fixed assets, such as cars and machinery, are worth substantially less than the original price once they are used. This progressive reduction in value has to be reflected in the company's accounts otherwise they would show a very misleading picture. The device used is to record a percentage of the value of such items as an expense each year under the heading of depreciation and the application of depreciation is referred to as writing down the asset.

Different rates of depreciation are applied to different types of capital goods, a ship may be considered to have a life of 20 years and so be written down by 5% per year whilst an office desk may be written down at 25% per annum.

You cannot leave the subject of how the value of an asset is shown in the company's books without touching on the subject of revaluation of assets. In shipping, perhaps more than most industries, the market is constantly fluctuating and occasionally these fluctuations are very great. Such fluctuations go beyond simply affecting the rates of freight being paid and spread their influence into the ship sale and purchase market. It would, therefore, be ridiculous if the owner steadily reduced the valuation of a ship in the balance sheet in accordance with a depreciation schedule while in the real world that ship had, perhaps, doubled in value.

Sadly the converse applies, the company would be lying to it's shareholders if a ship were shown in the books as only having reduced its value by, say, 10% when the recession was such that the ship had become worth only its value as scrap steel.

Revaluation of assets, up or down, is not carried out capriciously. A market trend has to be clearly expected to continue for a long time before any such action is taken and in many countries, company law has to be strictly observed.

To recapitulate, the Profit and Loss Account contains the sum of all the transactions over the previous year, the Balance Sheet shows what the company is worth at that particular moment.

11.5 MANAGEMENT ACCOUNTING

Reference to accounting so far, whether for use by the company or for official publication, has tended to look at the company's finances from a historical point of view. Management accounting looks at what is currently happening and what the company intends or hopes will happen in the future so that plans can be made to ensure continued or, better still, increased profitability.

Reference to the immediate past is still vital; you will often encounter the expression 'same period last year' when seeking a foundation upon which to set a guide as to the expenses this week, month or year. This forward estimation of expenses is a vital part of budgeting as, of course, is the parallel but often much more difficult job of estimating future income. Conscientiously using such systems of planning and checking is referred to as budgetary control.

Apart from all the obvious advantages of having as accurate an estimate as possible of the company's future fortunes, the ability to compare actual with budget at frequent intervals will give an early warning of anything going awry. In particular budgeting permits the company to forecast cash flow so that it can be sure it will have money actually available to pay expenses, from the smallest invoice to the highest salary, when they become due.

Most companies prepare management accounts several times a year, often monthly. They include a profit and loss account for the year to date and comparisons with both the budget and the previous year. They will also include cash flow forecasts.

11.6 CASH FLOW

Earlier in this chapter it was shown how, by comparing money due to come in with money due to be paid out plus money actually in hand, the company's profitability can be estimated. It does not matter how profitable the company is on paper, if the money is not physically available to pay vital things such as loan repayments, rentals, salaries and suchlike, the company will fail, become broke, go bankrupt or whatever term is chosen to describe total collapse.

It will be recalled that creditors are the people to whom your company owes money so, effectively, your company has some of their money in its account. Similarly debtors are those who owe your company money thus they have some of your company's money in their accounts.

If debtors have more of the company's money in their accounts than it has creditor's money in the company's account it will fast approach the stage when it has insufficient cash to meet immediate commitments, in other words it will reach a cash-flow crisis. Many otherwise profitable companies have failed due to mismanagement of their cash flow.

This is not a recommendation that a company should deliberately delay paying its bills well beyond their due date; a reputation as a slow payer can be damaging to future prospects. It is, however, important to negotiate the best possible payment terms with suppliers and to avoid conceding long credit periods with customers. Also important is having a person or department with special responsibility for credit control because slow payers can so easily become non-payers resulting in bad debts.

It might be assumed, if a company's accounts show a considerable surplus of creditors over debtors, that its cash-flow is in a healthy state. This may well be the case although such a situation could well be the precursor of a very unhealthy state of affairs such as falling sales which will produce a trading loss next year. You should not judge by a single detail in a company's accounts but always study all the different items.

Being able to show convincingly how healthy a company's future cash-flow position will be, is an exercise companies may often be called upon to do. If a bank or finance house is asked for a loan, the lender is primarily anxious to ensure that the borrower has the ability to repay the loan and meet the interest payments. Although a mortgage may be taken on, say, the ship as security for the loan, the finance house wants to buy and sell money, not become a shipowner. Thus before the loan is agreed the lenders will wish to study a cash-flow forecast or cash-flow projection which will have to persuade the lenders that they can be confident the borrower will be able to earn enough in order to meet its obligations under the loan.

11.7 COSTS

A capital asset such as a ship, once purchased, must be put to work in order to earn revenue and therefore profit. To do so will require expenditure on a wide range of items, all of which will have to be forecast as accurately as possible for budgeting purposes. To assist in this process, costs are divided into two basic categories: fixed costs and variable costs.

In the case of a ship you would easily distinguish between the two because fixed costs, as the name implies, are those costs which would occur even if the ship were standing idle. Loan repayments and interest on the loan are certainly fixed costs. A cost which also continues regardless of what is happening is depreciation because, as an asset grows older, so its value decreases, subject to any revaluation of course.

The expression variable costs is similarly self-explanatory. However, as your studies progress more deeply into the world of ship operations it will be seen that variable costs subdivide into running costs and voyage costs. Running costs are those that occur all the time a ship is operational, such as crews' wages, maintenance, insurance and suchlike. Voyage costs are those that apply uniquely to the voyage being undertaken at the particular time and will include, bunker fuel, port costs, stevedoring, agency fees and so on.

While fixed costs are there to stay, variable costs give wide scope for the skills of those concerned with budgetary control; careful financial housekeeping can make a considerable difference to the company's profitability.

Chapter 11

11.8 TYPES OF COMPANIES

11.8.1 Sole Traders and Partnerships

There is nothing to prevent an individual going into business on their own. In that way all the profit is retained, less what the Government takes as tax. The individual has to raise all the money necessary to operate the business which may mean borrowing money against a security such a house. Furthermore all the risks fall on the individual with the ultimate risk of losing everything, and even bankruptcy.

Two or more people may decide to pool their resources of money and skills and so form a partnership. Usually they draw up a partnership agreement which formalises the arrangement. The same benefits and risks apply to partnerships as to sole traders except they are shared according to the agreed terms. Note, however that if one partner is unable to fulfil its obligations, the other partner is obliged to bear full responsibility.

A partnership is usually referred to as a firm and partnerships are by no means always small affairs. Many firms of accountants, stock brokers and lawyers are very substantial but are still essentially partnerships.

11.8.2 Limited Companies

One way of avoiding some of the risks of sole trading or partnerships is to form a limited company. The thing that is limited is the liability. Those forming the company are shareholders rather than partners and their liability is limited to their shareholding; if the company collapses all they lose is what they paid for their shares.

Someone has to bear the rest of the loss and they are, of course, those to whom the company owed money. This seems hardly fair to any suppliers who provided goods on credit but it is a risk that is run when dealing with a limited company. However, this risk is lessened by the fact that limited companies are, in most countries, strictly controlled by law. They have to keep proper books of accounts and publish these each year via an official body. In the U.K. this is the Registrar of Companies.

Limited companies have to have Directors; at least two, who may or may not be major shareholders. The same set of laws that insist on accounts being published also set out certain terms of conduct to be adhered to by directors.

A limited company may be owned by a small group of shareholders in which case it is referred to as a private company and its name has to include certain prescribed words or initials after its name: The word Limited or the initials Ltd are used in the U.K.

Larger companies owned by a substantial number of shareholders are known as public companies and a different name or initials have to appear after their names appear. In the U.K. the initials plc standing for public limited company are used. As the name implies, public company's shares are available to anyone who wishes to buy them and they are traded on the stock exchange at whatever price the market puts on that company at the time of the sale or purchase.

Large companies may buy, or form, subsidiary companies which may themselves be quite large but as they will only have a few actual shareholders they are still private limited companies or Ltd.

11.8.3 Conglomerates and Multi-national Companies

Large companies can become what are known as conglomerates, which means that in addition to having several branch offices or factories they buy or create a substantial number of subsidiary companies. These subsidiaries may be in a line of business related to that of the parent or in quite a different trade. One reason for forming a conglomeration is for integration, for example a shipowner may have in its group of companies a trucking company so that it does not have to buy inland transport from another company. It may well have other subsidiaries such as a chain of agency offices so that it uses its experience to gain income from others.

Other conglomerates may be a group of quite diverse operations such as a shipping company, an engineering division, a timber division and so on. They may trade with each other but this is not the main reason for this type of integration. The object is usually to spread the risk. One year shipping may be good but the building trade poor so that timber is not so profitable. Another year may be a boom time for engineering but the shipping market rather weak. In this way the total profitability is maintained because it does not depend on just one market.

A conglomerate which establishes branches and subsidiaries both in the country where the parent is registered and in other countries enables it to trade throughout the world but retain the trade and the profits from that trade within its own organisation. This earns it the title of a multi-national and perhaps the best examples of such multi-nationals are the major oil companies as well as many of the liner shipping companies.

As referred to earlier in this chapter, to run successfully a company needs capital which has to be raised. The principal way to raise capital is to sell shares in the company. The shareholders will only invest in the company if they are sure of receiving income in the form of dividends which is the term used to refer to the distribution of profits to the shareholders.

11.9 EXCHANGE RATES

Each country has its own currency and each currency has its value in comparison with the currency of another country. Furthermore these relative values fluctuate. Later in your studies you may encounter references to a country's balance of trade which is the difference between what a country earns abroad with exports or services and what it spends abroad on imports. You could look upon the balance of trade as the country's profit or loss and this measure of its prosperity will have a significant, but not the only effect on the value of its currency against those of other countries. Other factors which impinge upon the complex foreign exchange markets are beyond the scope of this publication.

Those in shipping, being essentially an international business, constantly have to be aware of the effect that rates of exchange will have. For example, a company may have crews wages to pay in British Sterling, capital repayment in Japanese Yen, bunker and port costs in a wide variety of currencies and freight being earned in US Dollars. Any of these currencies becoming either much stronger or weaker or worth more or less against your own currency, could have a profound effect on profitability.

This effect is just as important to, say, a chartering broker whose own salary and communications costs are in the currency of its own country but as the freight is payable in, say, US dollars the broker's commission or brokerage, being a percentage of the freight, will also be in dollars. There is, of course, the paradox that if your own country is particularly prosperous just at that time and is enjoying a high rate of exchange in the world's markets, then the incoming dollar payment will yield less local currency than may have been hoped for at the time the deal was done.

When collecting freight on behalf of an overseas principal the effect of exchange rate fluctuations can cause a problem. If the agent in slow in remitting collected freight and the rate of exchange goes against the principal's country in the interim, the principal will suffer a loss, blame this on the agent's lateness and demand recompense.

One can cite problem areas relating to exchange rates in all aspects of shipping business which means that it is a topic demanding constant vigilance.

Chapter 11

11.10 COMPANY ACCOUNTS

Several references have been made to a company's published accounts and it is a worthwhile exercise to study an example to see how the basic elements of such a set of accounts might look. In practice a set of published accounts may also contain such things as a Cash Flow Statement as well as a list of Explanatory Notes which will include a description of the depreciation principles applied, the way in which assets have been valued and various other items.

Chapter 12
On board ship

Captain at work

Chapter 12

12.1 SHIP'S OFFICERS

Merchant ship's officers belong to three different departments:

- Deck officers;
- Engineer officers;
- Catering officers.

12.2 DECK OFFICERS

12.2.1 Watchkeepers

Deck officers are engaged to conduct watchkeeping duties on the bridge while at sea or at anchor and to undertake cargo watches in port. The deck officer is very highly trained. Depending on the country's jurisdiction, they spend three or four years at both maritime universities or sea schools and gaining sea-time on board ship. On completion of this training phase, the candidate sits a Class 3 certificate of competency. The main important subjects such as navigation and principles of navigation generally require a pass mark of 65-70%. Other subjects require 50-60% as a pass mark. Often there is an overall average of 65% required. The oral part of the examination generally requires a 90% pass mark.

Successful candidates are then judged to be suitably trained to start as a third officer on a ship. These officers normally stand the 0800-1200 watch and the 2000-2400 watch. They also provide mealtime cover for the other watchkeepers.

Watchkeepers on the bridge.

After a certain amount of sea-time, usually one to two years, the officer is eligible to study and sit for a Class 2 exam. This is very similar to the Class 3 except it is more complex. This exam replaced the old First Mates certificate of competency. It enables the successful candidate to work as a second officer or chief officer. The second officer is usually in charge of the navigation of the ship. Course lines on charts would normally have been drawn by the second officer, but approved by the Master. This is very much representative of the work of the bridge team.

After a further amount of experience at sea the watchkeeper can sit a Class 1 examination. This replaced the Masters Certificate and qualifies the successful candidate to command a ship. In practice there would normally be a period of work as first officer before the holder of a Class 1 certificate takes command.

12.2.2 Engineers

On the engineering side, Chief, second and third engineers normally commence their sea time with an engineering qualification. There is then a Class 3, Class2 and Class1 examination to be passed before the person can work as an engineer.

They work on machinery on board the ship in a repair or maintenance role. At sea they may stand a watch in the engine room control room. For a vessel with the notation UMS (unmanned machinery space) in its classification, the vessel's engines are supervised from the bridge.

Electrical engineers are sometime deployed on board to maintain and repair all the electrical equipment on the ship.

Cruise/passenger ships alongside.

12.2.3 Catering

Catering officers are generally given the term Pursers. Invariably they work on passenger ships such as cruise ships and ferries. They are in charge of the catering staff and are responsible for all the financial activities which take place on board.

12.3 MANNING

Vessels are manned according to international manning levels. Generally speaking a vessel requires a Master, a Chief Officer and two more watchkeepers. It requires a Chief Engineer and a Second Engineer and often a third engineer and an electrician. It needs cooks and stewards to feed the officers and crew and of course a sufficient number of deck and engine room crew to ensure that the ship can operate in safety.

It comes as a surprise to some in the industry that so few people can take some of the largest ships in the world to far-flung corners of it. Reports suggest that the Emma Maersk, currently

Chapter 12

the largest container ship in the world, operates with only 13 persons on board, but that the vessel has suitable accommodation for 30. This might be sufficient if everything is going well, but if there is a cargo fire on board, located deep in the container stack, the sea-going personnel might be seriously challenged.

12.4 INTERNATIONAL CREWS

Gone are the days when vessels flying the flag of a country employs officers and crews of that nationality. In an effort to drive down costs, ship-owners look to third world countries to man their vessels. The Philippines has a thriving manning industry. This has succeeded because after Tagalog, the country's second language is English.

Crews are truly international

Other Asian countries are also providers of officers and crews for merchant ships. Among them, Chinese, Indians, Pakistanis, Bangladeshis and Sri Lankans. If a ship-owner prefers European crew, these are often sourced from Eastern Europe.

12.5 APPLICATION OF REGULATIONS

Ships are guided by international, national and company rules and regulations. The most important of these are those promulgated by the IMO and the United Nations. These are regulations that prevent marine pollution (MARPOL), Safety of Life at Sea (SOLAS), law of the sea (UNCLOS), training standard (STCW) and collision regulations (ColRegs).

National regulations will include qualification rules and Port State controls. Although they are established by the IMO, traffic separation zones are policed by adjacent countries. Similarly, sulphur emission controls are also policed locally. Marine accidents are normally investigated by the flag state, but in the case of a serious accident involving loss of life, the local marine investigation organisation will be involved.

Ship-owning company-specific orders might involve weather routing, bunker safe-margins, maintenance schedules down to small details such as rostering and rest periods. Company policy varies to a great extent. In previous centuries, the Masters were very much in charge of their own little kingdom. The expansion of international communication networks has put an end to this and the degree of control a company exerts over its Masters can vary from loose to total.

12.6　A DAY IN THE LIFE OF A MARINER

Probably the day's work that a mariner performs varies from their rank to whether the ship is in port or at sea. We will therefore look at both scenarios.

12.6.1 Getting from A to B

The Second Officer is probably the officer we should study. They are middle-ranking, experienced and have a defined role on board. Before the vessel sails, the second officer (2/O) will have set up a passage plan to the next port. In the case of a ship navigated on paper charts, the courses will have been drawn with course alteration points marked. Usually these will involve navigating around a point or headland. The ship will be far enough away from the shore to be safe, but close enough to see lighthouses and other navigation marks.

Although chartplotters are becoming more prevalent, paper charts must still be used.

Chapter 12

Position plotting.

Tidal flows will also have a bearing on how far out to sea ship is. Generally speaking tidal flows are stronger further from shore.

On sailing from a port, 2/O's supervise the handling of mooring ropes and wires at the stern. They will be in touch with the bridge through walky-talkies or via fixed voice links. When the ship is clear of the berth and all mooring lines are stowed safely, the party will remain in place in case an emergency tug might have to be used. Otherwise if the ship is clear of the harbour, the 2/O will stand down. They stand watches on the bridge, usually from midnight to 0400 and from noon until 1600 hrs. At midnight the 2/O will go to the bridge and the handover will take place. The ship's position will have been marked on the chart or appear on the ECDIS screen. All other vessels in sight will be drawn to the attention of the relieving officer. Engine settings are pointed out and any special anomalies will be communicated.

Any Master's instructions will be passed on, there normally being a book of standing orders to be observed. The Master's special instructions may only be a large cross marked on the chart with 'CALL ME HERE' on it. Normally course alterations are carried out by the officer of the watch without reference to the Master.

If the ship is being navigated near a coastline, the vessels position will be marked on the chart and a note made in the bridge's rough log. The officer of the watch (OOW) will then guide the ship along its course, ensuring that a good lookout is kept. Away from land the ship's position, gathered by the satnav system will be marked at intervals on the chart. Such intervals will be set by the Master. Normally it will be once or twice in every four hour watch. On ocean charts, with a vessel proceeding at 15 knots, a sixty mile space in the course of a watch will be represented by a very small amount of progress on paper. The chart is likely to get very crowded.

At the end of the four hour watch, the 2/O will call the next watchkeeper, usually the Chief Officer and the normal handover will take place. The 2/O will then catch up on a bit of sleep and breakfast will normally be taken at 0800. The vessel's agent will have provided the ship with the latest Notice to Mariners booklet in which any chart corrections or temporary alterations

On board ship

to navigation marks will be included. One of the 2/Os duties will be to ensure that the paper charts are kept up to date. Increasingly, computerised chart plotters are the norm and chart corrections are downloaded in digital format and applied to the charts in the plotter's memory. Nevertheless the back-up paper versions must still be updated.

Taking nautical sun and star sights and calculating position lines is still part of the examination syllabus for watchkeepers. Some companies and Masters insist that junior watchkeepers keep their hand in by calculating the ship's noon position by sextant and chronometer. It is increasingly the case that sextants are stowed in their wooden cases on a high shelf or in a dark cupboard gathering dust.

Potential storms along the ship's course will be plotted and company instructions on the avoidance of such damaging natural phenomena will be observed.

The 2/O will also stand the 1200-1600 watch. The vessel may be big or it may be small.

Some vessels may be big or small, but each has its uses.

Nothing must distract the officer of the watch from keeping a vigilant lookout for dangers which usually amount to other vessels. This involves standing in the wheelhouse or on the bridge wing and taking a long hard look all around the horizon at frequent intervals. A radar is useful but a ship and its operation must never be treated like a computer game.

When the vessel is in port, the watchkeepers must team up and oversee the correct loading and discharging of the ship. The order in which holds are loaded must be balanced against the rate at which ballast can be discharged and the tanks from where it is pumped. Injudicious loading and discharging may result in hogging, sagging or shearing stresses which may contribute to shortening a ship's natural trading life.

Chapter 12

Chapter 13
Maintenance and demolition

Sparks flying

Chapter 13

13.1 DRY DOCKS

As mentioned in chapter 5, vessels have to undergo periodic drydocking. This is required under classification rules. These dictate that a vessel must undergo a special survey involving a drydocking every four years, but a year of grace is almost always granted. Should a vessel not adhere to this schedule it will drop out of class and become largely unemployable.

Dry dock in Singapore

From the time of delivery from the shipyard the maintenance clock starts ticking. After twelve months, the vessel has a guarantee docking where any faults that have emerged during the vessels first year of life are rectified. Before the ship's fifth birthday, the ship has the first of its special surveys. These continue to be required every five years thereafter.

In the harsh environment of salt water, heat and cold, rain, ice and snow, high winds and battering waves, a vessel's integrity is gradually comprised. Rust attacks the steel and plating gets thinner. This leads to steel renewals to keep the craft trading.

13.2 WHY A SHIP COMES TO THE END OF ITS WORKING LIFE

Eventually the renewals become so extensive that it becomes financially impracticable to carry on. Machinery may well need expensive replacements and ship's electrics and pumps may well be compromised by wear and tear and also become obsolete.

In the end it costs more to keep the ship in class and trading that it might be earning. The decision must then be made as to whether to sell the vessel into a less-strict regime, where standards are lower or sell it for scrap.

Maintenance and demolition

13.3 BREAKER'S YARDS

Scrapyards have been portrayed as forbidding places; a reincarnation of Dante's *Inferno*. The IMO has taken steps to improve safety and general conditions in the world's scrapyards, but it is an uphill struggle. In recent years, ships are run up on beaches on the Indian sub-continent at high-water spring tides and scores of workers tear it apart to gain every iota of value from it

Demolition beach.

All the steel is added to blast furnaces in the manufacture of new steel. The copper, bronze and brass are sold as cupro-scrap for recycling. All the ship is used and little wasted. And so the wheel turns a full circle and a vessel scrapped will be replaced by a bright and shiny new one. This is part of the supply and demand cycle with which everyone in the shipping industry becomes accustomed.

Chapter 13